The Monday Morning SalesCoach

By
Jim Dunn
&
John Schumann

Second Edition
San Diego, CA

The Monday Morning SalesCoach

Published by SalesCoach, LLC
6303 Muirlands Drive
La Jolla, CA 92037
Tel: (800) 235-2816

ISBN Number
1-931413-47-9

Printed in the U. S. A.

Table of Contents

3

Dealing With People

Strategies & Tactics

Introduction

The Monday Morning Sales Coach was conceived in 1998 as a way to reinforce training with our clients. The coaching lessons come from real situations that salespeople encounter.

It's important to mention that the selling methodology and tactics suggested here are most applicable in a more complex, relationship type of sale-one characterized by a relatively high financial investment, perhaps multiple decision makers and influencers, a longer selling cycle, etc. If you are selling a product or service that is typified by a one call close, low dollar investment, etc., some of these ideas may not fit in those situations.

You'll notice that the format for these "coaches" is Problem/Diagnosis/Prescription. This format mirrors the sales cycle as it should occur. First, the prospect should make a statement about the problem in general. Next, the salesperson should diagnose the causes of the problem. Finally a solution or prescription should be recommended. If that sounds like the medical profession, it's done purposefully. Too often, as you'll see from the stories we tell, the salesperson fails to complete the diagnosis before he or she begins to prescribe a solution. It's malpractice in medicine, and it's malpractice in selling as well.

Here we've stated the problem that the salesperson has encountered, offered our diagnosis as to the causes of the problem, and prescribed a solution. Diagnosis before prescription...the only way to sell!

As you read these stories we encourage you to do some self-examination. How often do you experience these very same sales challenges, and how do you handle them?

We'd like to thank Roy Williams, The Wizard of Ads, for the idea of sending a weekly lesson to our clients. Roy calls his the Monday Morning Memo. Obviously we liked his title. Dan Lucas also has been a positive inspiration and occasional contributor.

Our thanks also go to Candace Schumann for her wonderful suggestions regarding content and tireless editing assistance.

New coaches are written and emailed to our clients and friends on a weekly basis. If you'd like to be on our mailing list, just get on your computer and go to our website, www.mysalescoach.com. You can sign up for the Monday Morning SalesCoach there.

If you've experienced a selling situation that's not covered here, we'd like to hear about it. Just email it to us and we'll send you a response. If it's a good one we'll include it in our next issue of the book.

Good Selling!

Common Sense Selling

Problem: The other day we were working with a new group of people who had just started our training program and we were astounded at how difficult these folks were making the process of selling. We reflected on how everyone says that consultative selling (asking questions versus pitching features and benefits) is the way to go, but few can do it successfully.

Diagnosis: Clearly the old beliefs and habits had become so completely ingrained that they were preventing these folks from making the transition from a product oriented sales pitch to a discovery oriented process. Even with their notes in front of them, the urge to start selling at their first opportunity was so overwhelming that most struggled considerably with the new concept. And these were people who were experienced and in a relationship type of sale.

What was causing this to be so difficult? It stems from our belief system. There are several beliefs that, unless changed, will prohibit us from ever becoming a consultative salesperson that is able to effectively uncover the prospect's pain and suggest a targeted, value based solution.

Here's what those beliefs are.
"Our products and services are great and everybody in our target market needs them."
therefore,
"When they hear how good our stuff is, they'll want it."
but
"If they don't want it, I've failed."
therefore
"I need to work harder at convincing them to buy."

This is a completely logical thought process if the initial premise is true, but it isn't. This belief, however, can appear to justify behaviors such as overselling, talking too much, not listening, etc. Even if your solutions are great, not everybody needs them, no matter how good they are. (And just for once consider the possibility that your competition isn't so bad either.)

Wonder what would happen if the beliefs changed?

Prescription: Here are our rules for selling.   They're based on common sense.

Not everyone needs what you're selling. That's right, not everyone is a prospect.   So if you've qualified thoroughly and they don't need your stuff, "no" is okay. Ask yourself: "Do they really need my solution or do I need them to buy?"

You must understand a problem before you can suggest a solution. Prescription before diagnosis is malpractice. You should be asking yourself:
"Do I truly comprehend what the problem is, what's causing it and how it affects my prospect?"

There must be mutual trust for a relationship to be successful. When the prospect doesn't trust you, he may mislead you as a defense mechanism. You should know:
"Is what I'm doing now increasing or decreasing trust?"

In a successful sale, both parties win. Selling is not combat. If the prospect loses, eventually so do you in a sale where relationship is important. There can be no losers, real or perceived. Ask yourself:
"Is this a good deal for both of us?"

Try changing your beliefs, and watch your results change.

"Damn, I'm Good!"

Problem: Despite years of experience, attendance at numerous training programs and coaching from sales managers, many salespeople still fail to elevate their performance above the mediocre.

Diagnosis: Numerous factors can influence performance, but the most overlooked is attitude – how we feel about ourselves. Unfortunately, our attitude about ourselves, our self-image (self-confidence or self-perception) is influenced by our performance in our daily activities. And because our successes are frequently offset by disappointments, our self-image can be a roller coaster feeling. This causes an up and down performance in our roles, as you might imagine. You say to yourself, "Can I do it?" Some days the answer is "yes" and some days it's "no." It's key is to get your self-image raised to the point that the victories vastly outnumber the defeats.

Prescription: Think of any activity that you perform that you're really good at. It can be a sport, public speaking, cooking, organizing or anything. What is it that makes you so good at it? Is it your training, the tools you use or the experience you've accumulated doing it? It could be all of these things, in varying degrees, but something else as well. Your attitude, your approach, the sense of confidence and purpose, the commitment you bring to the activity is what people observe when they say you are "good at it."

Witness the athlete who makes the play so effortlessly, the actress who delivers her lines flawlessly. The athlete does so not because of any superhuman qualities, but because he has practiced and practiced, the actress because she has internalized the part. There is no longer any conscious effort required to make it happen. This is the difference between "knowing" it and "owning" it. Those who "own" it are at the very pinnacle of their professions.

When you marvel at the way someone makes a brilliant impromptu speech or plays a beautiful song on the piano without music you are marveling at the same thing – the approach, the confidence, the naturalness of the behavior. There was no time to think, no time to prepare, no time to hesitate. They just did it!

It all starts with a desire to accomplish something, then believing that you can do it, learning how it's done, practicing, practicing, and then practicing some more, until finally you don't even have to think about it – it just happens. You "own" it. But that takes commitment.

How good are you? How good do you want to be? Are you committed?

Top Ten Ways To Raise Your Self-Esteem

Problem: The best sales techniques in the world will not guarantee success in the selling profession without the proper attitude. Unless you feel good about yourself, you'll struggle to achieve your true potential. You must feel like you're a "10" if you're going to perform like one. And most people don't feel like a "10" most of the time. Here are a few ways to start improving your confidence, self-esteem and results.

Diagnosis: We are subjected to many negatives throughout our lives: missed quotas, reprimands, a bad golf game, argument with a loved one, etc. All are role related. And worse, we tend to internalize these negatives and let them affect the way we feel about ourselves. Think of all the negatives you get in sales: people don't return your calls, they lie to you on a regular basis, and, in general, treat you like a low life.

Prescription: We must understand that there's a difference between what we do and who we are. Our self-esteem must be separate from performance in our roles. How we perform in our roles does not define us as a person. So why beat yourself up if you have a bad day?

If you have a pet dog, you know that he's happy to see you every evening when you get home. He's not concerned about how well you did in sales that day. Fido always sees you as a "10" and is more than happy to demonstrate his affection for you.

Here's a few good ways to raise your self-esteem and raise the level of your performance in all of your roles as well.

1. Associate with people who have high self-esteem; some of it will undoubtedly rub off on you (if you let it).
2. Eliminate any negative influences in your life.
3. Take time to dream about the successes you'd like to have. Set specific goals and develop plans to help you achieve your dream.
4. Have faith that there is an abundance of everything that you need to be successful.
5. Become a giver; generosity will come back to you in many ways.
6. Read a good book (or listen to tapes) on self-development frequently. The bookstores and libraries are full of them.
7. Take the time to write down 100 successes you've had in your life.
8. Re-write the negative beliefs you've developed with positive affirmations.
9. Every day write down the good things that happened to you without regard to what you think the long-term repercussions might be.
10. Start behaving like you're a "10" now (in other words, fake it 'til you make it).

The Sales Charlatan

Problem: Have you ever heard the term "sales profession"? How about "medical profession"? Which one do you think has the most credibility? Of course, we're biased. We are those "professional" salespeople we spoke of a moment ago. But which would the general public, the people who are our prospective buyers, give the most credibility to as a real profession. Our guess is medicine.

Diagnosis: Medical professionals study for years before they are licensed to practice and then must undergo regular continuing education to stay licensed. The profession is highly regulated, and rightly so, since peoples' lives are on the line. But what about sales? The normal requirement to get into sales is often nothing more than an outgoing personality and a business card. Training ranges from nothing to rigorous, but usually is inadequate. Salespeople are often making recommendations on products and services that can have a profound impact on their customers. Yet, we have no regulating body to keep out the charlatans.

In medicine, they have a term for someone who prescribes medical treatment without an adequate diagnosis of the condition. They call that person a "quack". A synonym for quack is charlatan, described by Webster as someone who pretends to have expert knowledge or skill that he does not have.

How many "professional" salespeople prescribe a product or service before they've made an adequate diagnosis? Far too many according to the buying public. It's no wonder that, almost universally, salespeople are mistrusted. And it's no wonder that selling is so difficult, given that prospects don't trust salespeople.

Prescription: If you want to set yourself apart from your competition, if you truly want to be regarded as a professional, then begin with a better diagnosis. Tell the prospect that you won't give a presentation until you understand his situation completely. Then make sure you ask enough of the right questions to be able to suggest a solution that will completely fix the problem. That's what a professional does. You'll find you get more respect and sell more.

The Fallacy Of A "Full" Pipeline

Problem: Larry was a salesperson with 3 years experience selling printing services. He was constantly busy doing proposals and following up on the many prospects who regularly called him for quotes. Clearly, he had developed great relationships with his prospects and customers. While his sales manager was happy with his efforts (the company measured salespeople partially on their pipeline, which was the number of proposals outstanding), he was concerned about Larry's closing rate. To make matters worse, Larry seemed to have a severe time management problem and was just not able to find time to prospect for new business.

Diagnosis: Salespeople often think that they'll be successful if they make lots of proposals. Of course, it's difficult to get a sale without making a proposal, but a focus just on generating a large number of proposals typically causes one to shortcut the qualifying process. When a prospect is inadequately qualified, the closure rate drops significantly. It's a rare prospect who would decline a salesperson's offer to submit a proposal, even when they know there's only a slim chance that they'll ever buy. Prospects find it easier to say, "Thanks for the proposal, I'll look it over. Call me next week." And next week they have another excuse as to why they haven't made a decision. In the meantime, the salesperson's "pipeline" and expectations grow.

Prescription: Making a proposal is not selling. Anyone can make a proposal. In fact, if all a company wants to do is get as many proposals on the street as possible, they should hire someone for minimum wage and just churn out proposals. Salespeople must learn to qualify thoroughly before making a proposal. They must learn how to get a commitment from the prospect that if the proposal meets their needs, they'll give them the order. (Try getting this commitment without properly qualifying.) Fill your pipeline with quality, not quantity.

Come To The Edge...And FLY!

Problem: Salespeople have difficulty "breaking out" of their comfort zones. Despite increased activity (usually in frantic spurts), trying new techniques and approaches, and resolving that things will be better next month, things somehow manage to stay pretty much the same, and results show little or no improvement.

Diagnosis: What you see as "reality" is defined by your comfort zone. Envisioning success beyond the bounds of our current reality is difficult for most of us. In fact, we're often blinded by what we think is reality but which is simply a reflection of our past.

Prescription: Understand that life and true success starts at the edge of our comfort zone. Getting to the next level (perhaps a level of success which you have difficulty even envisioning at this point in your career) requires stretch, discomfort and vision. Don't be held back by your lack of vision.

As the French poet/philosopher Guillaume Apollinaire wrote:

> "Come to the edge."
> "We can't. We are afraid."
> "Come to the edge."
> "We can't. We will fall!"
>
> "Come to the edge."
>
> And they came. And he pushed them.
> And they flew.

Learn how to fly.
You can, you know.

All Pro Or Peddler?

Problem: Picture your last very important sales interview with Mr. Big -- the one that potentially represented three months quota. You know the one we mean. Going into the meeting, on a scale of 1 to 10, where would you rate yourself on the following scale? One means your briefcase is full of literature to show him, and 10 means that you have planned the call well and have rehearsed the questions you will ask to help you understand the problem in a way that fits with Mr. Big's behavioral style and frame of reference. If you scored less than an eight, your chances of a successful meeting are less that 50%.

Diagnosis: Winning the big deals in professional selling comes from believing in and executing a set of strategies and tactics that allow you to handle any selling situation in an optimal way. It is similar to professional sports. Some athletes think they know the game but the top professionals know that it takes continual training and preparation to give them a slight edge in the big game.

Prescription: Prepare yourself mentally and emotionally for every sales call. Visualize, practice and rehearse critical components of the interview. Know exactly what you want to say to set the agenda for the meeting. Know precisely how you will transition to the pain step and what questions will be relevant to the prospect's organization and situation. Study the prospect's behavioral style and modify your approach accordingly. Anticipate the "tough" questions you may get asked and prepare an appropriate response or question. Writing out the playbook doesn't hurt either. A peddler wings it. The pro is prepared.

Excuse Making

Problem: Bert, VP Sales for ABC Company, was explaining to the CEO why they were 50% short of goal. "Our prospects tell my salespeople our pricing is 25% higher than our closest competitor, business is terrific so why risk change, and they (the prospects) don't understand Web-based e-commerce yet." Bert continued, "I can relate. We are pretty new. Maybe our goals are too ambitious." Ms. CEO replied, "Those are all probably good reasons, but it's your job to make goal, so deal with it." (The CEO presented similar reasons to the Board of Directors for being off target.) Bert accepted that these were serious issues that had to be dealt with and worked with his people to make more effective calls. However, the environment didn't change. Customers continued to have challenges around ABC's solutions. ABC ended the year 50% off projection, Bert was gone and the new Sales VP took a new approach.

Diagnosis: The sales culture of this company was severely debilitated by a tendency to blame external factors for their lack of results. We call that not taking responsibility or making excuses. The problem's severity was compounded because ABC did not recognize this as a major problem. Each time the folks at ABC accepted external-factor excuses as valid reasons for lack of performance, this problem became more habitual and rooted in the sales culture. The CEO, the sales manager and the salespeople blamed the product, the pricing, the marketplace, new concept, etc. Many of the excuses were cloaked in shreds of validity and were easy to accept as factual and as real reasons for lack of success. ABC did not consider excuse making unacceptable. No one coached the salespeople on how to recognize and deal with their own excuse making.

Prescription: The company must immediately make a cultural change. It must stop accepting excuses and start coaching their sales professionals to recognize when it is happening and what to do about it. Awareness must precede change. The new sales manager should search for "excuses" when debriefing sales calls. When presented with reasons a customer will not move to the next step or is stalling, she might ask the salesperson, "If there was a another reason why the prospect is not going forward, what would that be?" Or, "Aside from that reason, what are some of the other reasons you think the prospect doesn't like our solutions?" Then the sales manager could follow with, "If you had surfaced that in the sales call, how would you have dealt with it?" Then, "What do you think would have happened? Would that have changed anything?" This type of coaching empowers salespeople to hang in there and work harder and smarter. If everyone recognizes when folks are blaming external factors for lack of sales success, change happens and people start taking responsibility for outcomes. From the CEO down, everyone should listen for excuses, look for excuses and point out excuses. When excuse making is not acceptable in a company, there is a positive supportive growth-oriented environment. The comment, " Are we making excuses?" is welcomed as a barometer that guides us toward increased earnings and shorter selling cycles.

Looking Down On
Your Meeting

Problem: In the parking lot on the way out of the sales meeting, Sid shook his head and said to his manager, "If I would have only asked about..... the call would have taken a favorable turn. Why can't I think of those things while I am in the middle of the meeting?"

Diagnosis: Salespeople get emotionally "hooked" by reacting to what a prospect says during an interview. The emotions could be anything from despair ("I'm losing this") to exhilaration ("things are going great"). For example: a prospect denies that they have a problem that you may be able to solve or challenges your credibility. This triggers an unconscious thought pattern that generates a feeling of frustration or defensiveness. This emotional response happens unconsciously and occupies our thoughts for a period of time. During that period we can't ask questions, listen properly or be objective. When a salesperson becomes emotionally involved in a meeting, they have lost control and will not be able to function effectively.

Prescription: Visualize yourself looking down on your meeting. There is a scientific term for this called dissociation. Dissociation can be learned and it starts long before you show up for the sales meeting. First, learn a system that will provide you with an overall strategy and set of tactics to handle any selling situation in an optimal way. Practice, rehearse and review it so you can follow it faithfully (like you would any other skill game or sport). This gives you the ability to focus on the process of the meeting rather than the outcome - a key element of dissociation. Secondly, build your conviction and understanding by affirming these key concepts:

- Approach a sales call as if you had just won the lottery and you don't <u>need</u> the business.
- Remember that people buy things for their reasons and not for your reasons, so find out what their reasons are.
- "No" is an acceptable result of a sales call (provided you have qualified properly).
- Selling is no place to get your emotional needs met - get your emotional needs met from those who love you and support you.

How Good Is Your Sales B.S.? (Belief System)

Problem: Jeremy had been selling for 15 years and was feeling a little frustrated lately. He honestly evaluated his job in sales and figured out that there were some things about selling that he really hated. Top on the list were: chasing prospects who don't return calls, wasting time doing proposals and presentations for prospects who shop around, always having to work hard to convince prospects, dealing with resistance, and handling constant rejection.

Diagnosis: His belief system (what he believes to be true) is the cause of the elements of his selling career that he hates. Most salespeople have learned to believe that a "no" from a prospect means failure and, that to be effective at selling, it is necessary to give polished, convincing presentations and be good at overcoming objections. Maybe worst of all is the belief that prospects will tell the truth in a sales interaction all of the time.

Prescription: Attitude (your belief system) is the key to success in everything you do. Change some of your non-supportive attitudes and adopt a system of beliefs that are consistent with success in selling in today's competitive markets. Here is our top five:

1. I have no money worries and don't <u>need</u> this particular piece of business.
2. My job is to disqualify people who aren't prospects.
3. "No" is okay (as long as I've qualified properly).
4. If I sense something negative, bring it up with the prospect (politely).

5. It is the prospect's job to convince me that they have a problem and it is important enough to do something about it.

Adopting these beliefs will provide a new outlook on selling and your career.

The Law Of Detachment

Problem: Jason was extremely excited when he finally got an appointment with one of the top prospects in his territory. The first meeting went extremely well. So well, in fact, that he felt that he was a lock to get the business. He saw this prospect as his ticket to making his quota for this year and the next. Finally, he'd be getting out of his sales manager's "dog house" and even having a chance to make his company's "Heavy Hitter's Club". He told everyone who would listen about his good luck. He was, to put it mildly, very attached to this piece of business. He just had to get it. However, it began to unravel and a competitor won the account. Sound familiar?

Diagnosis: Sometimes things fall apart because we want them too much. It's called being "attached" to an outcome. It is based on fear and the insecurity of not having something. It does not mean that you give up the goal, the intention or the desire. The unfortunate mindset is that we desperately want that piece of business and will be deeply disappointed if we don't get it. That's the surest way NOT to get it.

Prescription: Detach yourself from the specific outcome, but have total faith that ultimately your goal will be achieved. That's a sign of security. Understand that there are an indefinite number of possibilities between point A (today's reality) and point B (tomorrow's goals). If one opportunity does not materialize, another will. Try this for a belief system: "I will make my sales objectives, I just don't know for sure exactly which of my prospects will be signing purchase orders, but it will happen." As a belief system, this will empower you to maintain a positive attitude regardless of the outcome, and will keep you focused and motivated.

Singing The Santa Claus Blues

Problem: The holidays are a curious time of year for salespeople. They tell us that after the Thanksgiving holiday something strange starts happening. It seems as though they're not able to contact as many prospects, make as many appointments or close as many sales. If you sat in a room full of salespeople discussing the matter, you might get the impression that Santa Claus was public enemy number one!

Diagnosis: There are two schools of thought here. The first is that the whole idea of the slowdown in activity is in your own head. It's kind of self-fulfilling. Initially you don't believe it when your colleagues tell you that things are slowing down. You demonstrate your positive attitude and deny it. Within a short time, after a few unsuccessful attempts at cold calls, it is remarkable how quickly you become convinced that your colleague's assertions are true. The next thing you know you catch yourself telling someone else that things are slow because of the holidays.

In contrast, the other prevailing point of view is that there truly is a slowdown this time of year and it has always been that way. The salespeople who believe this do so because they keep track of their activity ratios and can prove it if challenged. In writing about this, we are not concerned with what school of thought you believe in as much as what you do about it.

Prescription: Here are two ways to handle the Santa Claus blues. First, challenge yourself to overcome your "head trash" and keep your prospecting efforts up. If the majority of salespeople are thinking that nobody will talk to them, there will be less competition for attention. Your results will improve and at the very least you will have planted some good prospecting seeds for next year.

The second way to tackle the problem is to use the extra time you have now to do things you normally don't have time to do. One example is setting goals and mapping out sales strategy. Another could be to write those lead generation letters you always wanted to write. Join in the festivities. Invite your best clients to lunch and have some fun while improving your relationship, maybe even talking about some business opportunities for next year. It's critical to maintain a positive mindset. You are in control of how you deal with reality and what actions you take. Why sit around singing the blues when you can get an edge on sales for next year?

Dealing With Rejection

Problem: While in my office the other day, I got a call from a financial advisor. As soon as I answered the phone he began a pitch that lasted for what seemed a very long time, listing all the reasons why I should do business with him. I told him that my wife controls the investing in our family and that she has had a successful relationship with a competing broker for over 20 years. Although the guy pressed harder, I sensed that I took the wind out of his "sales" when I said, "Look, I'm just not interested." My eardrum rattled as he slammed the phone down hard. This was likely followed by some derogatory reference, most likely directed at me for rejecting him.

Diagnosis: First, and I won't address it here, his phone tactics were just plain *awful*. They needed some serious polishing. But for the moment, let's assume his phone tactics were adequate. The main problem was that the salesperson reacted to the call with a feeling of rejection. That bad feeling probably transferred forward into the next few calls. I suspect that it might have taken this person a little longer to recover.

Prescription: There is no rejection here. Was I a good prospect? The answer is, "No." I haven't made a buy or sell order for years. I have little input at my house on investment decisions. Did I reject him? No, I didn't even know him. I didn't have any need for what he was selling. He did his job. He disqualified me and put a line through my name. If he felt anger and rejection, it was because he created it. He is the one who decided to take my response personally. Disqualifying prospects is a very important and productive part of prospecting. Remember, you must sift through a lot of dirt and rocks to find some gold nuggets.

In other words, it is okay to feel good about disqualifying a prospect as long as you have used proper selling tactics.

Six Bucks An Hour

Problem: A typical week includes activities like: calling existing customers to check on their orders; following-up on all pending proposals; drafting proposals for prospects who fax in requests; reading the business journal; updating the contact database; creating ideas for the new web page; scheduling training and conventions; going to the printer to get promotional materials printed; writing letters; attending association meetings; and, holding strategy meetings for getting more clients. Everyone's busy but sales don't seem to be reaching potential.

Diagnosis: You could pay someone to do some of the above activities for six bucks an hour. In addition, many of the above activities are easy to do and may be interesting but they are not productive selling behavior.

Prescription: Stick to the fundamentals. Productive selling behavior could be worth $500 per hour or more. Don't believe me? Do some quick math. Divide your income last month by the actual number of hours you invested in productive selling activities (which only includes direct prospecting, qualifying interviews, and presentations). These ideas may help you improve your selling behavior:

- Ask for referrals from the existing and past clients you have served well.
- Know what you need to do and track it while you are doing it. Keeping score will help you stay focused on your vital activities.
- Challenge yourself by setting a goal for the number of prospecting calls you will make per day or week and do them. Know your numbers and don't wimp out.

- If you must do other activities, create deadlines for them. Keep a log on where your time goes and then fix what isn't productive.
- Remind yourself that everything you do should be directed toward talking to more prospects. You are not really working if you are doing anything else.

How much minimum wage work are <u>you</u> doing?

Be Careful, You Might Get What You Wish For!

Problem: Every year in most major cities there is a road show consisting of prominent self-help gurus and other personalities who spend a day telling the audience how to feel good about themselves and improve their performance. Most of the audience is in sales. No surprise! Sales is a tough business, rejection is commonplace and pressure to meet quotas can be unrelenting. It's no wonder that salespeople have attitude problems. While these events are useful in momentarily motivating attendees, what happens after the motivators leave town? After a few days, most folks are right back in the same mess as before, and little has changed. So how can we make change permanent?

Diagnosis: Although these workshops are helpful, long term we are responsible for our own attitudes. How often do we silently proclaim, "I can't do that", "I'll never be able to..." or worse, "I don't deserve..."? How often do we set goals and expectations at a "safe" level so that we can be assured of making them? The person who wants to play it safe, who is hesitant to get out of his comfort zone, may lead a comfortable life but may fail to achieve his true potential.

Prescription: "Imagination rules the world", declared Napoleon Hill. Albert Einstein (that's right, old $E=MC^2$) professed, "Imagination is everything, it's a preview of life's coming attractions."

Much has been written about how we are a product of our thoughts. Essentially, we are a self-fulfilling prophecy. The mind brings into reality the things it thinks about most. However, our subconscious mind makes no distinction between positive and negative thoughts. If we fill our mind with doubt, fear and disbelief, if we lack self-confidence, if our self-image is negative, chances of our being successful are remote.

We gravitate in the direction of our dominant thoughts. This is an extremely important principle. Think about something and you will move toward it, even if it is something you don't want. Therefore, saying "I don't want to blow this opportunity" or "I better not miss this shot" often will cause us to achieve the opposite of the desired result...in other words, failure.

We get what we expect. That's good news since we are in control of what we think about. You decide what to put in your mind and so determine what you get back. Discipline your thoughts and you'll determine what you reap. "The average man quits at the first failure. That's why there have been many average men and only one Thomas Edison", remarked Napoleon Hill. How true these words are.

I've Just Won The Lottery, And I Don't <u>Need</u> The Business

Problem: How many times have you run into a salesperson who pushes too hard, who epitomizes the pushy, aggressive stereotype that we've come to loathe? These folks can't accept a "no" from a prospect and think their solution is the right thing for everybody.   They generally appear desperate to make a sale and usually are. This aggressive approach works okay in a very simple transactional type of sale since we'll sometimes buy just to avoid an argument or to get rid of the pest (oops, I mean salesperson).   But in a more complex sale, this approach is fatal.

Diagnosis: The real world, however, is that often we are under tremendous pressure to make the sale.   And although we may hate to admit it, we are desperate occasionally. The little man inside is saying to us things like, "C'mon, you need this sale to make your quota this month.   You'd better push a little harder; be more enthusiastic.   Sell, sell, sell."   As you listen to this self-talk, something changes in your approach to the prospect.   You start to come across as needy, pushy and aggressive.   You also begin to notice a change in your prospect.   No longer is he open and agreeable.   Instead, he's defensive and protective of his turf.   Your behavior has had just the opposite effect that you wanted.   And often this is where the sale is lost.

Prescription: Well, traditionalists won't like this advice very much, but then most of those folks aren't very open to new ideas.   Let's pretend for a moment that just before you had gone on that sales call you'd stopped at a convenience store and picked up a lottery ticket...and it was a winner. A million bucks!

You had finally achieved financial security!

With the winning ticket in your pocket do you think your attitude on that sales call would change much? Yeah, I know. You wouldn't go on the sales call. But if you did, would your attitude be different? You bet it would. Think you'd come across as desperate for the sale? Not hardly. Instead you'd be able to exude a quiet confidence that only a financially secure person would have. Your prospective buyer would notice that attitude and be more comfortable with you and the call would probably have a better result. Try adopting a new attitude ("I've just won the lottery and I don't have to make this sale today.") and watch your fortunes change. I promise, they will!

Just The Facts, Ma'am

Problem: The results of a recent study conducted by The Sales Board confirmed what we have known for some time. Prospects are speaking up about how they feel about salespeople who are less than professional. We thought that you would like to see these statistics as they reinforce the need for a sales process and challenge you to improve your qualifying efforts.

Diagnosis: The study showed the following startling facts. Can you relate to them as a salesperson or as a buyer?

Fact: 82% of salespeople fail to differentiate themselves from their competition.
Result: They lose the business, fail to sell value or don't get their price.

Fact: 86% of salespeople ask the wrong questions.
Result: They miss selling opportunities and end up wasting time while appearing unprofessional.

Fact: Only 18% of salespeople close without discounting price.
Result: Discounting becomes a habit and profit margins are eroded.

Fact: 95% of customers say salespeople talk too much.
Result: Customers are bored and feel salespeople don't care about understanding their problems.

Fact: 62% of salespeople do not earn the right to ask questions.
Result: They fail to position the sale properly and don't gain commitment.

Fact: 85% of salespeople use a selling process that is extremely ineffective, compared to the buyer's system.

Result: They close less than 50% of the business that they should close, with disastrous effects on their companies' sales and their personal incomes.

You may be "winging it" if you find yourself relating to any of the following: (a) chasing prospects who don't return calls; (b) hearing "think it over" all too often when you ask for the business; (c) cutting price in an effort to obtain or keep business; and (d) spending most of your time in front of people who are not decision makers.

Prescription: 1. Stop assuming that your prospect needs what you're selling. 2. Learn how to ask more questions to see if the prospect has any serious "pain" issues that your product or service can resolve. 3. Learn a sales process to help you stay in control of the sales interview. (If you don't know where to go to find one, call us We can help.)

Missed Those Goals...Again!

Problem: Sarah told me her goal for the past year was to lose weight and get in better shape. Bill's goal was to increase his sales. Nadine was going to reduce her credit card debt. Sarah, Bill and Nadine all had something in common. They all failed to achieve their goals. At the end of the year, in fact, none had even come close. And all were frustrated.

Diagnosis: People start out with the best of intentions regarding goals. But most goals go unrealized because they were doomed from the start. People who fail to achieve their goals do so for several reasons: lack of commitment, poorly written goals and/or no plan to make it happen.

Prescription: First, the goal has to be important to achieve. You need to understand the personal benefits of achieving the goal (as well as the negatives of failing). Second, goals must meet the **SMART** criteria. In other words, they must be **S**pecific, **M**easurable, **A**chievable, **R**ealistic, and have a specific **T**ime frame to complete the goal. For example, Bill's goal might read, "I will generate a 25% increase in sales in my territory by the end of the year." Simply increasing sales is not good enough. Is the goal achieved if Bill gets a 15% increase? Finally, what is the plan to make it happen? What specific activities will be done and when will you start?

Don't make the mistake of failing to achieve your goals again next year. Start the New Year off right. Be committed. Write SMART goals and have a plan. If you don't, then plan to fail.

"Makes Sense To Me"

Problem: Krista had been making a lot of sales calls, seeing many people, and enthusiastically presenting proposals during the past few months.   She was pleased that her pipeline was full because she had so many proposals on the street.   Her prospects seemed to take a lot of time to make buying decisions.   The problem was that sales were just not materializing.   Krista did not believe her colleagues when they told her that her prospects were not being totally honest with her and to expect only 5 to 10% of her proposals to turn into business.   Krista believed that it made sense for her prospects to mull over their decision because she sold a complicated high tech solution.

Diagnosis: Krista has what we refer to as a non-supportive buying process.   This refers to the process by which a salesperson makes purchases for themselves.   In this case Krista's method of buying typically involved going to several vendors, collecting lots of information, and spending a great deal of time evaluating which option to choose.   Krista used this process for virtually every purchase over one hundred dollars.   As a result, she tolerated behavior from her prospects that were similar to her own.   She often commented that she "understood" why they needed to take their time to evaluate her proposals, but as a result she was vulnerable to stalls, put offs, lies, excuses, sob stories and other forms of "think it over's" from her prospects.   It's called buyer empathy, and it has no place in sales.

Prescription: The only answer to this problem is to change the way Krista makes her purchasing decisions.   When her buying process begins to support her selling process, the stalls and put offs that used to derail her will begin to disappear.   Instead of being understanding when her prospects want to take a lot of time to make a decision, she would begin to question why and would become more comfortable asking them to make a timely decision. Once this self-limiting belief system is addressed, Krista will be able to shorten her selling cycle since she will expect quicker decisions from her prospects.

Get rid of your buyer empathy and watch your sales increase.

"You Haven't Heard The Best Part"

Problem: Jim and Howard were presenting their case for doing business with one of the largest grocery retailers in the U. S. Their company, Lincoln Inventory Services, sold inventory counting services to retailers. Associated Grocers represented an important sale for them. About halfway through their presentation Sam, Associated's CFO, said, "Okay guys, you've said enough. I can see that your program will meet our needs. We'd like to sign the contract and get started immediately." Jim, the sales manager, relaxed visibly. They had done it; they bagged the big one; it was over.

Suddenly Howard, Jim's local sales rep, said, "Wait a minute, Sam. You haven't even heard the best part." Intrigued, Sam replied, "What would that be?"

Howard then proceeded to launch into a discussion of Lincoln's warranty program, stating, "If Lincoln ever conducts an inaccurate inventory, we'll come back and recount it at no charge." Howard was really proud of the warranty program.

Well, Sam's response was predictable. He asked, "How many bad inventories do you guys do? Tell me about your quality control program."

Suddenly, Jim and Howard found themselves in a discussion about quality with Sam, who was now skeptical of Lincoln's ability to count inventories accurately.

Diagnosis: Howard had committed a cardinal sin of selling: when the sale is made, don't offer additional

43

information as it can often cause you to lose the sale. Unfortunately, Howard was of the old "feature & benefit" school of selling and found it very difficult to keep his mouth closed. He felt that the additional warranty information would help solidify the sale, when it had just the opposite effect.

Prescription: You're in the sales profession, not the education profession! Sellers are not teachers and most teachers can't sell. Often we hear salespeople say that they need to educate their prospects; and as a result, they spend far too much time dispensing information. Product knowledge is mistakenly considered to be the "holy grail" of selling. The fact is that product knowledge used at the wrong time can be devastating. In Associated's case, a seemingly positive bit of information caused the buyer to raise an objection and the sellers to go on the defensive.

Howard and Jim recovered, but Howard almost got a very expensive lesson. Sell today. Tell them about the warranty program if and when you need to use it. Product knowledge is used to address the prospect's pains, not to provide a variety of reasons to buy from the seller. When you've got the business, keep your big mouth shut!

Rather Make A Friend Than Make A Sale?

Problem: Stacey and her boss just couldn't understand why she continued to struggle to make quota. She was a very outgoing person who was extremely well liked by all her colleagues and her customers. Stacey constantly went out of her way to be friendly to everyone and appeared to possess a good knowledge of both her product and the selling process. Her failure to excel was confusing to everyone.

Diagnosis: A major weakness that many salespeople have is called "need for approval". This means the salesperson's need to be liked is stronger than the need to close business. This need to be liked is very common and causes the salesperson to be overly polite and to avoid any confrontation. This also means that they will be unlikely to ask the tough but important qualifying questions and will rarely risk testing a prospect's commitment level before preparing a presentation. More acute cases of this weakness cause salespeople to avoid hearing a no at all cost and accept too many stalls and put-offs. These salespeople unconsciously get paid in compliments rather than in dollars. Extroverted people often suffer from this weakness as they value personal relationships greatly and are loathe to do anything (such as asking for the business) to upset that relationship.

Prescription: Research suggests a salesperson with a need for approval will be about 35% less effective than someone without this major weakness. Overcoming the need for approval can be a difficult problem but it can be overcome with proper reinforcement and commitment to change. Here are several ideas to consider that will help to reduce the need for approval:

- Be aware that selling is a highly paid profession to advance business goals, not a social event. The purpose of sales interactions is to collect information about prospects by asking qualifying questions. Selling is no place for meeting your personal needs (wanting to be liked and showing how much you know).
- Remember that it doesn't matter what anyone thinks of you, says about you, or feels about you. The only two things that matter are that you have fun and get a qualified prospect to do business with you.
- Get comfortable with hearing "no". "No" is an acceptable response when the prospect does not qualify to do business with you and you have done a good job asking questions to draw out the information you need. Learn to help people say "no" rather than put you off.
- Learn to ask the tough qualifying questions to get information you really need. For example, it may not be comfortable to ask about money, details of the decision-making process or to test commitment, but you have to do it.

Remember this quote from the famous actor Bill Cosby, "I don't know the key to success but the key to failure is trying to please everybody."

Instant Success?

Problem: Paul was an average performer in his company and marveled at the incomes and status of the top performers.   He had been to a few one-day seminars and read a book on motivation but it didn't seem to be working fast enough for him and his motivation was decreasing. He complained frequently and was thinking about moving on to a better opportunity so he could make more money.

Diagnosis: There seems to be pressure today to get results quickly.   The media publishes stories regularly of people who became "overnight successes" without paying their dues like most people. People become programmed to think that if they are not one of the overnight successes they are experiencing failure. The truth is that overnight successes are very, very rare and that's one reason why they become newsworthy. These stories create unrealistic expectations and cause anxieties that hinder progress. The result is that people "give up" or "move on" when a more focused effort and greater conviction could help them break through to a higher level.

Prescription: There is no such thing as instant success in selling and/or growing a business. Achieving excellence is an ongoing process.   It starts with a desire to accomplish something significant and demands patience during the process. You should create a picture or written description to remind yourself regularly of what your goal is and your plans to achieve it. If you can see it, you can achieve it.

Now comes the hard part. You develop true conviction not only by thinking about what you want, but also by taking action toward it.   Accept the reality that you will have to do things that are uncomfortable, tolerating failures on the road to success and using them as positive learning experiences. Understand that successful people are constantly pursuing knowledge. Begin a program of learning cutting edge selling strategies and tactics that will give you an edge on your competition. Associate with positive people and engage a coach to guide your progress. Constantly reinforce what you learn by practicing and repeating the key skills until they are second nature and you don't have to think about doing them. Commit yourself to success and do what it takes to get there. Be a winner, not a whiner.

What's A "No" Worth?

Problem: One of the most common requests we get is for time management training. It seems there just aren't enough hours in the day for most salespeople. Companies spend big bucks for cell phones and PDA's so salespeople can stay in touch and on customer relations management programs to make them more efficient. Training programs are conducted to help them evaluate areas where they are wasting time and provide solutions. Yet they still have time management issues.

Diagnosis: Unfortunately, the biggest time waster of all for salespeople is being overlooked. What is it? You guessed it...the ubiquitous "I need some time to think this over. Call me in a week or so." Salespeople still have a problem getting their prospects to make a decision when they make a presentation and that stems from the fact that they just hate to hear "no". So, they permit their prospects to drag them through the purgatory of alternating hope and despair, just because they don't have the intestinal fortitude to hear a "no".

Prescription: Face the facts. You know that most "maybe's" are just slow "no's", so why not get the "no" in the first place. Get rid of your old head trash. You don't have to sell everybody. Ain't gonna happen. You and I both know that.

Let's look at the problems with "think it over's" and "maybe's". It takes forever to get a "no", which permits the prospect to steal your valuable time and employ his system at your expense. The slow "no" causes pipeline and forecasting problems (how much of your current forecast is wishful thinking?) It gives you a false sense of security,

49

but when it becomes apparent that there will not be a deal, it's devastating.

Here are two additional suggestions to eliminate "think it over's". First, make sure you discuss that at the end of the meeting you'd like to talk about the next step, assuming you're both in agreement that the dialogue should continue, and that your prospect understands that he doesn't have to string you along just because he assumes you're not comfortable hearing "no." Finally, your attitude on every sales call should be: "my prospect must convince me that there is a reason for my continued involvement in the sales process." In other words, if you're having any doubts that there's a reason for the two of you to do business together, tell that to the prospect. Let him convince you that he really does have a problem and that you should stay involved.

So what's a "no" worth? Just the most valuable thing you possess: that irreplaceable asset, your time.

The Marquee Account

Problem: Tony was looking for advice on how to sell a high profile prospect who was constructing a large new distribution center in his territory. Tony's company sold and installed voice and data cabling and new construction was its primary market. Tony related that the buyer insisted that the business would go to the vendor who had the best price since they regarded voice and data cabling as a commodity so clearly price would be the only real buying criteria. That, unfortunately, would virtually eliminate Tony's company since they were definitely not the low price alternative. He said he had probed extensively for pain and found none. The actual dollar value of the business was not great and Tony said he wanted to focus on better prospects, but Bill, his sales manager, was adamant that he continue pushing to get this business. Tony felt that his only real alternative was to drop the price and "buy" the business, but he was afraid they'd lose money on the deal. He felt trapped.

Diagnosis: Most business owners, sales managers and salespeople have their wish list of "marquee" accounts that they are desperate to have on their customer list. Having high profile accounts is a great idea, but some of these companies should not be on anybody's list. Sometimes they are just too difficult to do business with. However, this blind obsession often overrules good judgment. People become emotionally involved in selling these prospects and find it very difficult to take "no" for an answer. So they often offer concessions that do not make good business sense and they invest far too much valuable selling time trying to close the deal. While they're doing this they run the risk of neglecting existing customers, making costly concessions and missing some real opportunities for lack of time.

Prescription: Obsession may be a great name for a perfume, but it has no place in the world of sales. The more emotionally attached you are to a piece of business, the less objective you'll be. Have you ever rejoiced after you won a big, high profile deal only to regret it later? If it's not good business for you, let your competition have it. (Letting them deal with low margin, problem accounts actually might be a good business strategy.) You should evaluate every piece of business on its merit, and if makes good business sense, go get it. Don't obsess with a big name account just because of the marquee value.

It's The Numbers, Baby

Problem: A few months ago, one of our clients complained that they were not achieving their quarterly sales goals. Many proposals were outstanding and sales forecasts seemed to be bloated with deals that showed up month after month, but never seemed to close.

Diagnosis: In the case of this sales team, the main problem was that they had developed a serious case of cold calling cowardice. The symptoms of this deadly affliction are fear of rejection, need for approval, failure to prioritize, lack of concrete goals, procrastination and spending too much time on unimportant activities. In short, they found every excuse not to prospect. They had lost sight of the goal which was to focus on the prospecting activity and forget the results. And, they had developed a severe reluctance to hearing "no" from a prospect.

Prescription: We had to break it down to the basics. We looked at what the monthly sales goal was, determined what an average sale was, and concluded that they closed about 20% of the people they were able to get an initial appointment with. Another important number was the number of calls they had to make in order to get a first appointment. With this information, we determined that they each needed to make about 9 cold calls (defined as any attempt you make to speak with someone who might be able to buy your product or service) per day...every day. And based on the fact that at least half the attempts resulted in a "NOH" (no one home), these 9 attempts typically could be done in less than an hour a day. We also discovered that based on commission structures and closure rates, every attempt to speak to a prospect was worth about $27.50 to the salesperson. We decided that each salesperson would devote one uninterrupted hour per day, in the morning, to this effort. When they had made their nine attempts, they could reward themselves with a Starbucks or something like that. The key to success was to understand that every prospecting call paid dividends and that every "rejection" they received was a success.

Oh yeah. Their sales increased by 34% the next quarter and they all cashed more commission checks!

.

A Prospecting System That Guarantees Results!

Problem: A large majority of salespeople struggle to get in front of enough prospects to keep their pipeline full. As a result, they feel desperate, have a difficult time dealing with rejection, and often avoid asking the tough questions to find out if they really should be spending their time with someone. This leads to a long selling cycle, inefficient time management, and ultimately, failure.

Diagnosis: Prospecting is a tough business, the drudgery of selling. Most salespeople have not developed an effective behavioral prospecting system and even worse, fail to stick to the system that they have. They see prospecting as having little reward.

Prescription: Here's a great idea! Every day, put yourself on a 20 point activity system like this one:
- 1 point for a telephone contact with a decision maker who can tell you "no!"
- 1 point for a "customer service" call on an existing client.
- 2 points for forcing a decision to a "NO".
- 2 points for setting an appointment.
- 3 points for getting a referral.
- 4 points for a face-to-face meeting.
- 5 points for a sale.

Whatever you track will improve. Earning points gives you a target that lets you can "earn" a reward. You can modify this system to fit your situation if you want, but don't quit until you get your 20 points. Find a way to reward yourself when you accomplish your goal. Keep in mind that you'll always feel good if you do the right activity.

(Thanks to our old friend John Condry, Career Success Seminars, for this idea.)

"I Can't Think of Anybody Right Now"

Problem: Tom heard that getting referrals was the easiest way to get new customers.   So he selected 20 of his best clients and called them.   He was pleased that almost all of his clients said they would be happy to help him.   The problem was that he didn't actually get any introductions. What he did get was a very common response that sounded like this: "I can't think of anybody right now.   I'll have to get back to you".

Diagnosis: When you ask for a referral, you are asking for a response that can require a great deal of thought.   You are asking someone to intellectually identify with what you do and who you do it with, then sort through their own database of people, who they know and what they do, then analyze past conversations and select a few names.   This is often expected in a few seconds and can create a little psychological pressure.   That is why people generally choose to ask for time to alleviate the pressure.   And, of course, when the pressure is off, your request is forgotten.

Prescription: Pressure will cause people to become uncomfortable and end the dialogue.   The key to avoiding this problem is to guide your client through this referral asking process in a gentle and nurturing way.   Getting referrals is an emotional communication process with several questions and steps.   The first step is to get your client to remind himself that your past relationship has been positive and that there is nothing that you have neglected that could be improved.   Secondly, ask for their permission. This might sound like, "How would you feel about referring people to me?"   Since 80% of the time you will get a positive response to this question, proceed by thanking them and explaining the reason why you are asking for their help. Remind your client of what you do and whom you do it with by restating your introductory pain probe. Gently ask who they know who may have one or more "pains". You may even have to help by gently suggesting sources for the names you are looking for like associations, golf partners, social groups, competitor companies or suppliers. When your client gives you a name, don't forget to thank them. Ask for more information about the prospect and an introduction. Remember to respect that your client has agreed to help you and they may feel they are going out of their way. Psychologically they will need to feel good about the whole process. Referrals are the best way to get more clients when you know how to do it right.

Are Some Prospecting Calls Just A Waste Of Time?

Problem: Jenny came to sales training class one morning and asked the class to assess what had gone wrong on a sales call that she had made the week before. She was frustrated that she had spent 45 minutes on one call with no results. She explained the call in detail and after a short, but very focused Q & A, it was determined that the "suspect" she had spent her time with was not a good prospect after all. Jenny reluctantly agreed, but said that this happened more than she liked, and lamented that "some prospecting calls are just a waste of time", With that admission, she received much sympathy from some class members who agreed with her perspective on prospecting. Jenny admitted that her prospecting activity had declined in recent months and that she was no longer the leading salesperson in her region.

Diagnosis: Depending on the industry you're in, some, perhaps even many, prospecting calls lead to a dead end, to be sure. Unfortunately this perceived "failure" can lead to the conviction that prospecting efforts are, indeed, a waste of time. That perspective starts to affect the salesperson's attitude. What becomes perceived as a reality can become a self-fulfilling prophecy, and slowly, but surely, the prospecting activity starts to decline, and with it, the sales results.

Prescription: Don't permit "unsuccessful" prospecting calls to affect your attitude about one of the most important functions in selling. Nobody bats a thousand and in selling, it's the number of attempts that's important. Every prospecting call pays dividends. An old trick they used to teach in insurance sales was to keep track of the number of prospecting calls made and divide it into your income. While the results would vary by salesperson, one might easily find that every call was worth ten or twenty dollars. So if you knew that you were actually "getting paid" for each call, no doubt you'd be inclined to make more calls. Remember, every time you dial the phone to make a cold call, you make an investment in your success. Every call pays dividends. Now go make some cold calls.

Beware Of What You Send Before Your Meeting

Problem: Dennis was the VP of Sales for a medium sized application service provider and was concerned about the high number of appointment cancellations his reps were getting. As an example, he related something that had happened about ten days before. Apparently Richard, one of his reps, had made an appointment with a prospect that looked like they'd be a good fit for the company. A day after the appointment had been made, the prospect called back and asked that the rep send "some information" about the company prior to the meeting. Richard felt that this was a good sign of interest and complied, sending a fairly extensive package of information. It contained spec sheets on some of the products, a partial client list, company history, several recent news releases, etc. Then two days before the appointment was scheduled, the prospect called and cancelled, saying that they had looked over the material that was sent, and they felt that a meeting would not be necessary. This, explained Dennis, happened too often.

Diagnosis: You may find this hard to believe, but often prospects are looking for a way not to meet with you. We've all had meetings with salespeople that have proven to be disappointing and afterward said to ourselves, "Well, that was a waste of time. Wish I'd qualified them better before I let them come in." So, they want to see something first and often they're using what you send to disqualify you. Does this mean that they'll always find something they don't like? Of course not, but think of what Richard sent: specification sheets on products that might not be a fit; a client list that might not contain similar type companies or companies that were too small or a company history that someone could interpret as not having a "good enough" track record. You never can tell.

Prescription: Beware of what you send to prospects before you meet. The ideal situation is not to send anything, to let your skills in asking questions and probing for the prospect's pain give them the desire to see you. But if you must send something, ask them what they want to see and find out why that's important. And, send a very minimum amount of information. In this case, less is better. Finally, tell them that you know they'll undoubtedly find something in the information that may not apply to their situation and that you hope they won't use that as a reason to have second thoughts about seeing you. You'll find that simple statement will make them think twice about finding something to disagree with.

Sounds Like You're Busy

Problem: The following frustration was shared with me the other day. "I made contact with 127 potential prospects this week and only 8 of them gave me the time I needed to tell them what I do. The rest of them said they were busy and did not have time. I have been taught that prospects are concerned that salespeople will take up too much of their time so I always ask if they have a few minutes to talk. What do I have to do to earn a minute of time?"

Diagnosis: In today's fast paced business environment it is uncommon to find a prospect who is not busy and pressed for time.   In fact, people who have too much time on their hands are generally not good prospects. In a cold calling situation, when people are faced with the question, have you got a minute?", there's sufficient psychological pressure to generate a response like "No, I'm busy".   This negative response is predictable 80% of the time. Looking at it from a psychological perspective, it is a form of emotional stroke for a busy person to reinforce how important their time is to an unknown caller. Once making the decision to state how busy they are, a prospect is likely to support that decision by ending the call.

Prescription: Asking a negative question will produce better results and a more truthful response early in a telephone call. And, it will improve call ratios. Start a call as usual by stating your name and your company with appropriate tone, pace, and articulation (very important), then ask the negative question.   Appropriate questions might be: "Sounds like I caught you at a bad time?" or "I get the feeling I caught you in the middle of something?" (Again, delivered with appropriate deferential tone, pace and articulation).

The difference with this approach is subtle. If the prospect responds with, "Yes you did", then you get credit for respecting their time. Yet often they'll tell you when to call back or ask you what your call is about so they can decide whether or not to speak to you. At this point you can give them your introductory pain probe to see if they will speak to you further. This approach is different enough that when executed properly, it will help to earn you a minute of time with more prospects.

Death Of A Salesman

Problem: Most salespeople hate cold calls and aren't very good at making them. As a result, cold calling activity is limited and they never seem to improve. We all get cold calls on a regular basis and most result in failure. See if you can relate to any of the following.

Diagnosis: The first 10 to 15 seconds are critical in a prospecting call and will set the stage for success. Most prospecting calls shriek "SALESPERSON CALLING" and trigger the prospect to turn on their automatic defense system. All of us have heard one too many sales pitches and tricky one liners. Here are some examples of how salespeople unconsciously shout "I'M A SALESMAN" in the first few seconds of a call. In parentheses is what the prospect is probably thinking.

- "Do you have a few minutes to talk?' *(Oh sure, I was just here in my office wasting a little time)*
- "I'm calling to tell you about our new_____ " *(Big deal, I don't need it, don't want it, and I don't care.)*
- "If I could show you a way ____" *(This guy must have just attended one of those weekend training seminars.)*
- "We're giving away a free _____ with every new customer." *(Sure...what are the strings?)*
- "We are announcing a new.... (and in to the pitch)". *(Can I just get a word in edgewise to tell you I'm not interested?)*

Prescription: Don't act like a salesperson! Break the pattern. Your task, once the prospect answers the phone, is to create a respectful, low key, and non-threatening environment. Have the courage to ask if you got them at a bad time. Tell them it's a sales call. Ask them for 20 seconds to tell them why you called. Promise to be brief and right to the point. Tell them you may not have anything they'd be interested in and that it's okay for them to tell you if they have no interest. Don't act too friendly or familiar.

The purpose of your call is to determine if there may be a reason to do business together. There may not be. In order to find that out, you have to get them to talk to you. This approach will help you do that.

Gatekeepers & Screeners: Roadblock Or Asset?

Problem: Mike's company had developed a new product line and, for the moment, his primary responsibility was cold calling to develop a list of prospects. Mike's last serious cold calling activity was a few years ago and he remembered the frustration involved with trying to get past the gatekeepers. Today it seemed even more difficult getting to the decision makers and the gatekeepers' skills were undoubtedly more effective. Now those memories were flooding back and his enthusiasm for making these calls was fading quickly. He was under some pressure to get results quickly and that was adding to his frustration.

Diagnosis: Mike's difficulties were a result of his old sales programming. He was trying everything in his power to get "past" the gatekeepers, from pretending to be the decision maker's friend, to trying to bully his way through. Those approaches hadn't worked very well back in the old days, he remembered, but he figured his experience would make the difference. It didn't. Nothing was working.

Prescription: Doing things the same way over and over and expecting different results is insanity, as we know. So let's look at the reality of the situation. Gatekeepers (defined here as the decision maker's personal assistant) all have one thing in common: they know the boss better than you do and are often privy to company policies, vendor relationships and other information that can be helpful to the salesperson. So why not leverage that asset? The screener/gatekeeper can help you immensely, if you'll let them. Next time you've got the screener and can't get through to the boss, try this simple, yet effective approach.

Politely and briefly tell the screener why you called and what your product or service does. Ask the screener if s/he thinks it's something the boss would be interested in. You may find out quickly that it isn't and, if so, I'd move on. But if it is, ask how to best communicate your message to the boss. You'll save yourself lots of valuable prospecting time with this approach, improve your knowledge of the prospect, and your next call won't be a cold one.

Sound Like A Salesperson?
Get Ready For Rejection

Problem: Jason was new to the company and was trying to develop his territory. He didn't lack enthusiasm and was making his objective of 100 cold phone calls a day. He felt pretty good about that since he saw others make far less. But still, he was not making nearly enough appointments to keep his pipeline filled and wondered how he was ever going to achieve his income goals if things didn't change.

Diagnosis: Unfortunately, Jason was committing an error common to most salespeople. His cold calling approach sounded like every other salesperson. You know, something like this…"Ms. Smith, this is Jason Jones with ABC Company. We're a leading provider of software solutions and I'd like to tell you how our products can help you save time and money." CLICK! The ugly sound of rejection. Most salespeople's approach is so familiar that the prospect simply goes on automatic pilot, tunes the salesperson out and looks for an opportunity to end the call.

Prescription: Try to keep the prospect off balance. If they don't know where you're coming from or where you're going, it's difficult for them to control the situation. Since the first 7-10 seconds of the call are critical, a more effective approach would be to start by saying something like this, "Hi, Sue, this is Jason Jones. You're probably not familiar with my name." Prospect will say she is not, but wonders if she should be, so is not thinking about how to get rid of you. You then continue with, "That's okay, I didn't think you would be. Listen, I've got to tell you. This is a sales call. I'll bet you're filled with excitement and anticipation. And you probably want to hang up." (She won't.) Then instead of pitching your features and benefits, tell the prospect the kinds of pains you solve for your customers and begin qualifying, and always remember to tell the prospect it's okay to say "no."

You could keep making your cold calls the same way you've always done; just don't expect the results to be any different. Try this approach for a change of pace and see if your results are any different. We'll bet they are.

.

Referrals Going Nowhere? Upgrade Them!

Problem: Most salespeople certainly don't get enough referrals and often the referrals they do receive go nowhere. How many times have you called a referral, failed to get through the gatekeeper, and left a message that never gets returned?   Perhaps you've even gotten through to the referral, only to be met with a cool response?   We all know that referrals are the best source of new business, by far, so why does this happen?

Diagnosis: First and foremost, salespeople don't ask for enough referrals.   There are several reasons for that. Sometimes it's perceived as a "begging" activity, and few of us want to be seen as needy.   The second reason is that they have experienced poor results in the past when calling referrals.

Here's what often happens.   The salesperson is thrilled just to get the name of a referral and sprints to the phone to make what amounts to another cold call.   Often the referral hasn't heard of the salesperson or her company or was simply doing the referring source a favor by saying, "Okay, tell her to call me."   Then he put it out of his mind.

Prescription: Upgrade the quality of your referrals.   Ask your referring source to do just a little extra work for you. When you get a referral, ask a couple of quick questions to upgrade the referral.

First question.....
"Why do you think so and so would be interested in my product/service?"   This will help you understand what the prospect's pain is.

Next question.....

"Can I ask a favor? Would you feel comfortable calling so and so and telling him a little about my company and see if he's even interested in talking to me?" 90% of the time the referring source will be glad to do this.

And finally.....

"Thanks. When can I call you to find out if so and so will talk to me?" This puts the ball in the referring source's court to turn the "cold" call into a "warm" call. And the referring source, since he's close to the prospect, usually will strongly urge the referral to take your call. If the referral doesn't want to speak to you, you don't have to make a cold call that is probably destined for a negative result anyway.

Now when you call the referral, he's familiar with your name and is expecting your call. Here are a couple of questions to break the ice. "Mr. So and So, this is Mike Smith with ABC Company, does my name ring a bell?" His answer will tell you whether or not he remembered his conversation with the referring source. Next question: "What did Jim tell you about me?" Or, "why do you think Jim wanted me to call you?" These questions will take all the pressure off you and get the prospect talking.

From there, based on his answers, begin to ask your qualifying questions and try to get an appointment if the pain is real and he wants to fix it. The bottom line is to get your referring source to do a little more work and your referral business will increase tremendously.

"May I Ask What This Is In Reference To, Sir?"

Problem: When Sam, the salesperson, heard the familiar question from the other end of the phone, a shiver went through him as if he had scraped his fingernails on one of those old green blackboards. He was taught that you had to push past the executive's gatekeeper, giving little information because the person screening the call couldn't buy from you, only get rid of you. His typical response would be," My company is Powerful Services, Inc. and I would like to talk to Mr. Bigg about some concepts that will pay huge returns". He was usually put on hold for a second and then told that Mr. Bigg was in a meeting, followed by "Could I take a message or put you into his voicemail?"

Diagnosis: People who answer calls directly for high level executives in large companies are empowered to guard against unimportant callers and interruptions that could steal important time from Mr. Bigg's packed workday. Salespeople who attempt to push past the telephone screener fail to realize the significance of the Executive Assistant's role in the organization. The Executive Assistant is often an experienced and respected member of the company with high-level skills and with access to privileged information. Salespeople who do not provide the proper level of respect or use manipulative techniques to avoid the screener may be doing so at their own peril.

Prescription: The Executive Assistant (EA) may be one of the most important people you will ever talk to in your prospect's company. Stop thinking of getting past them. Start thinking about how to work with them to get the information you need. One of the simplest ways to start is to verbally acknowledge that the EA does play an important role in keeping unwanted interruptions away from Mr. Bigg. The EA often is aware of the problems the boss is working on and will actually help you if there is a belief that you may be able to help. Use your rapport and questioning skills to work with the screener and you may eliminate that horrible sensation the next time you hear, "What is this in reference to, Sir?" Remember that the EA is trained to keep out salespeople who make self-centered pitches and do not show respect, but not people who may have something of value to help the company.

No Secret Formula

Problem: Many salespeople wish there was a secret formula to prospecting successfully for new customers. We often hear salespeople moan, "If only more people would listen and talk to me. We know they would buy our service".

Diagnosis: Prospects are bombarded with sales messages and buying opportunities. One recent study estimated that on average each of us is exposed to more than one thousand messages every day. Add to this the complexity and pace of business, prospects have no real way to cope but to screen out much of what they hear and see. Further, prospects buy for their own reasons and at the time that is right for them-not for your reasons or timing.

Prescription: Follow these fundamental rules of prospecting for business:

1. Make a one-hour appointment with yourself every day to prospect. This takes discipline and is easy to put off. Don't.
2. See the end before you begin. Clearly identify the sales results you want and lay out the steps or "campaign" on how you will accomplish it.
3. Develop your cold call script and introductory pain probe that fits with your prospecting activity and the objective you want to accomplish in your call. Refine your script frequently to maximize results.
4. Research and create a list of your most likely prospects and make as many calls as you can. This improves the quality of calls. More calls are always better than less.
5. Keep calls brief (no more than 2-3 minutes). Remember the purpose of your call: to find out if the

prospect has enough pain to warrant spending time with you to talk about it.

6. Work without interruption. The more you prospect, the better you get and the more momentum you will have. The hour will fly by.

7. Call during off peak hours to take advantage of better times to reach your prospects and to avoid times when high volumes of other calls are being received by your prospects.

8. Be organized and keep records of whom you called and what was discussed. Schedule the timing of callbacks so you don't miss them.

9. Stay with it. Sustained effort and positive activity leads to results. There are no exceptions.

10. Reward yourself when you accomplish your prospecting goals. Positive reinforcement helps you sustain the effort.

A New Twist On Getting Referrals

Problem: What salesperson gets an adequate supply of referrals? Most don't. For most, getting good referrals is a matter of chance, not choice. And yet, referrals are the best source of new business. Without referrals, salespeople are dependent on other prospecting sources such as cold calling, and cold calling is the least productive of new business development efforts.

Diagnosis: Why aren't salespeople more proactive in asking for referrals? There are lots of reasons and it all boils down to what the experts call "negative self-talk". It's also known as head trash and it sounds like this: "What if I ask for a referral and they don't have one? Asking for referrals will make me appear needy. Every time in the past that I've asked for referrals it's turned out to be a futile effort. Getting referrals sounds good, but the reality is that it doesn't work." With this mindset, one can imagine how difficult it is to ask for referrals.

Prescription: Here's a new tactic for you to try. Often we invite customers to lunch or dinner. When the date is set, say this to your client: "Can I ask you a question? Let's pretend we were having lunch next week and during the lunch I brought up the subject of referrals. That'd make you uncomfortable, wouldn't it?" The odds of your client saying, "Yes, you're right", are very low. Chances are they'd say, "Oh no, that would be okay." A gentle takeaway ("Are you sure?") will confirm their willingness to give you referrals during the meeting. Now you've set the stage to ask for referrals during your appointment. Once the stage has been set, discussing whom they might be able to refer you to will be easy.

Sending Information?
Mutilate It First

Problem: Marketing departments have a love/hate relationship with salespeople. They "hate" them (sometimes) because they feel their products and services would sell more if the salespeople knew what they were doing, but they love 'em because they are great consumers of all the product literature, brochures, fliers, etc. that marketing departments tend to crank out. Let's face it, salespeople still have a tendency to send information to prospects every chance they get. When a prospect says, "Send me some literature", most salespeople interpret this request as sincere interest and are optimistic that they've got a "live one". But rarely does mailing literature result in a positive outcome. Prospects deny receiving it, plead they haven't had time to read it or simply don't return the salesperson's calls.

Diagnosis: Although most salespeople are beginning to understand that a literature request is often a put-off, they still have a tendency to send it. Why? First, most prospects disguise indifference in an attempt to get rid of salespeople. "Send me some literature" gets most salespeople off the phone quickly. Secondly, hope springs eternal. Salespeople feel that if the prospect gets the information and actually reads it, the "compelling" sales story may get a positive response. Finally, no one likes rejection. No appointment and no next step (like sending literature) is a "no" – rejection. "Got to avoid this at all costs", the little guy inside our head tells us.

Prescription: Our recommendation is to avoid sending literature unless you have a really compelling reason for doing so and have a good meeting agreement with the prospect as to what will happen after he receives it. If you absolutely have to send literature, make it easy for your prospect to read it. Mutilate it!

You want the prospect to look at enough of the information to understand your message and want to read more. Here are some tips for getting your literature read. Mark important passages with a brightly colored green highlighter (decision-makers are often driver types and green attracts their attention, surveys show). Take a bold felt tip pen and draw arrows to important things and write, "read this". Use post-it notes for added emphasis. Attach your business card with the back (blank) side showing and write on it "here's the info you wanted me to send". All of this says to the prospect, "Read me, I'm different." With all this clutter, it would be difficult not to get noticed and you're saving your prospect time by making your message easier to read.

Water Your Referral Tree

Problem: One of the hallmarks of a successful salesperson is the number of referrals they get from past customers and others. Many salespeople do not get enough referrals to keep them from having to make cold calls and do prospecting on a regular basis. Often salespeople do not get repeat referrals because they fail to water their referral tree.

Diagnosis: People who refer business to you need to be recognized for their efforts. After all, they have gone out of their way to help you become more successful. There is a time-tested principle that states, "an unrecognized behavior does not get repeated". Sometimes salespeople don't even know where their referrals come from.

Prescription: To water your referral tree, here are some ideas:
- Call the referral source and thank them.
- Send a thank you note or a gift.
- Keep them informed of your progress (as long as it is not confidential) until you close the sale or close the file.
- Ask your new client (the person who was referred to you) to call the referring source and thank them for the introduction.
- Make a point to refer business back if you can.
- Meet with the referring source and create a mutually beneficial plan to help each other. Not all referral relationships are balanced, so think of other ways to make it a win-win.
- Hold social events that include your best referral sources and prospects.

- Keep referral sources on your newsletter or other client communication list.

Why should you do all this? Unless you love cold calling, it's the best way to grow your business.

Why Should They Give
You An Appointment?

Problem: One of the biggest challenges that salespeople face is getting appointments. People are constantly bombarded by marketing messages via the media enticing them to purchase. Prospects receive daily calls from salespeople who want to see them, so it's no wonder that they treat most requests for meetings with skepticism and suspicion. This unfortunate fact of life makes the salesperson's job that much more difficult.

Diagnosis: Basically, the prospect isn't clear as to why she should see you. She's been promised so much from so many over the years, but the results have typically been less that promised. You are viewed as an unwelcome intruder who must fight an uphill battle just to get the appointment.

Prescription: There are several things that you can do to give yourself an advantage. First, deal with the skepticism and doubt up front. Tell the prospect what you will not do. For example, "I will not waste your time making a bunch of promises about how my product can help your company. The fact is I'm not sure we can help you, but I'm calling you because many other companies like yours have found that our product has been a good fit for them. Do you think it would be worth 30 minutes of your time to evaluate something that has the potential to...(mention a pain you can fix or a benefit they might receive)? If at the end of the meeting you don't think we have a fit, I'll be on my way. Does that sound fair?" This can be done over the phone or even adapted to an email or a letter.

Another option is to tell them what they will learn by meeting with you. Make reference to a satisfied client who received measurable results from your product or service that are meaningful to this particular prospect. "At the very least, you'll find out just how people in your business are successfully dealing with...and you'll discover some realistic options to change how you ..."

Remember, no one likes the typical sales BS and no one likes surprises. Be up front and tell it like it is, then deliver on your promises.

Another Bloated Pipeline

Problem: Roger was in a bind. Every month, his five sales people reported the "pipeline" of business that they thought would convert into sales for the next month. He then summarized the report for the president of the company. At the last meeting the president told him that his report was "bloated with deals that just seemed to roll over each month" and that "he'd better get it right next month, or else".

Diagnosis: Salespeople tend to be an optimistic group. When they hear the prospect say, "Great presentation. Give us a few days to think it over and get back to you", they often believe that they have a good opportunity that deserves to be in the pipeline. Many sales people want to avoid a "no" at all cost and have convinced themselves they have a solid prospect even when they don't. Salespeople often do an inadequate job of getting prospects to share the implications of their problems, their budgets and decision-making process. This combination of optimism and inadequate qualifying causes salespeople to revert to chasing prospects and to pest-like behavior, leaving those futile ("Could you give me an update on where we are?") voicemail messages.

Prescription: First of all, a "no" is an acceptable outcome on a properly executed sales call. A salesperson has to be willing to accept a "no" when the prospect is not qualified or when their offering does not fit. At the end of a qualifying interview with a decision maker, a salesperson should be able to ask this commitment question; "Assuming I came back with a solution and you had the conviction that we have the right solution for your problem, and it fit in the budget that we discussed, what would happen then?" If you get a positive response you can put it in the pipeline. If you get any other type of answer, you've still got work to do.

In summary, here is what you need to keep a prospect in your pipeline:

- The prospect has convinced you their problem is important enough for them to fix - and you know you can fix it.
- They are willing to invest the amount of money with you to fix it - and you can do it for that amount.
- They have a date that is important to them to have the solution in place - and you can do it in that time frame.
- They are committed to taking action if you can demonstrate that you have the right solution.
- You have a date for a presentation to get a decision

Networking... An Opportunity Or A Waste Of Time?

Problem: Have you ever gone to a networking function and spent 60-90 minutes or more and left without one good, qualified lead? If you're like many salespeople who sell, you can undoubtedly relate to this type of lost opportunity. Networking functions are a great way to meet people you can do business with, but typically we are disappointed with the results.

Diagnosis: Think about how you spend your time at networking functions. Many will spend their time with a friend, safely inside their comfort zone or take the easy road and meet only one or two people, failing to get a lead from them. Why does this happen? There are lots of reasons, but the main one is that we're uncomfortable in networking situations because it's a sales situation. We're asking someone for a lead and are afraid we'll be perceived as being pushy. We ask, "How can I get some business out of this? Who can you refer to me? What if they say no to me?" The focus is clearly on us.

Prescription: Change the focus! Focus on the prospect. Find someone whom you know you can help. Approach them with the idea that you have someone to refer to them (of course you must actually have someone).

Here is what it might sound like: "Do you have a moment? I'm _____ with _____. My company does _____. I think I have someone who could use your product/service, but I want to make sure. Can you tell me a little more about what you do?" After they've had a chance to talk, you can offer them the referral, if it's appropriate to do so. In either case, they'll be appreciative that you wanted to help them and I'll bet that they'll be thinking about how they can help you. It is Emerson's Law of Compensation in action which, when simplified, states: "the more you give, the more you will get in return." Obviously, you may have to do some preparation beforehand, but you can bet that the effort will be rewarded.

Create The Atmosphere

Problem: A year or so ago, we recall having a disagreement with a prospective client, Susan, on the subject of "pain". We agreed that the concept of pain was valid in that it focused on the needs, wants, challenges, etc. that the prospect was facing. There was no argument that the sales interview should focus on the prospect's pain and not on the product's features and benefits. Where we disagreed was on how the pain was developed in the first place.

Diagnosis: A well-known sales training firm had trained my prospect. Their position relative to pain was that the salesperson's job is to "create" pain...even if none existed. Susan was a real "driver" personality and her philosophy was that any sales call that did not result in a sale was a failure. The training she had received fit well with her personality style and she accepted it as gospel. So, in order to make a sale, she would often employ an extraordinary barrage of manipulative and aggressive tactics. This inevitably made prospects defensive, destroyed rapport, and she became very dissatisfied with her results.

Prescription: First, we had to refocus her attitude toward what the goal of a sales call really was. When she agreed that not everyone was a prospect (a real leap of faith for her) and that she'd be happy if she were simply able to get far enough in the relationship to ask the right qualifying questions, she had made her first significant step in the right direction. Then we discussed creating an atmosphere where the prospect was comfortable discussing their pain with her. She learned to do an effective meeting agreement where she got permission to ask questions in order to understand the prospect's issues better. She even became comfortable telling the prospect that it was okay to say "no" if it didn't look like there was a fit. She learned to tone down her aggressive style so that the prospect wasn't threatened. Doing these things helped create an atmosphere where the lines of communication were more open and her results improved dramatically. It began with an attitude change, followed by some solid technique and her sales *greatly* improved!

The Babble About "The Best"

Problem: Talk to many salespeople today and you may hear some familiar babble. "We have the best _____ in the market today." You fill in the blank: best product, service, quality, pricing, technology, research, etc. You know the script. You may even have said it yourself. Instead of being impressed, most prospects respond to such claims with remarkable indifference.

Diagnosis: There are at least three issues with babbling about being the best that create problems in the sales interview. First, your claim may be untrue. Of course, you are not intentionally making false claims but if you are in any competitive business (and who isn't?), there are usually worthy competitors who offer comparable - or better - products and services. The second problem is that you sound like a traditional salesperson which scares the heck out of most prospects. Think about how you feel when you are being sold. Finally, and most importantly, your prospects couldn't care less about your claims until they discover how they might impact them personally. They care about themselves, their issues, their dreams, their goals and their world.

Prescription: Get the prospect to reveal their world to you before making any claims. Stop telling, stop assuming and start asking. Ask questions to help a prospect discover what their concerns are and to demonstrate that you care about them. As soon as they recognize that you are more interested in them than yourself, rapport will increase and they will be more likely to open up and share the real issues with you. Next time a prospect asks you why she should invest in your product or service, try responding with a disarmingly honest answer: "That's a good question. I don't know enough about you yet to know if there is a match between what I have and what you need. If you would be open to sharing a little about your situation with me, maybe we can see if there is a fit. Sound fair?" By being the "best listener" you will experience the magic of a receptive prospect.

Mixing Like Oil & Water

Problem: Mike, an experienced rep who sold computer software, prided himself on being a results-oriented, take charge guy who was able to close effectively and get his customers to make decisions quickly. He felt his strength was to show prospects how his product would help them reach their business goals. He liked to get right down to business and disliked discussing the technical aspects of his product, both from a specification as well as an application point of view.

Mike was very comfortable dealing with most CEO's, but was often frustrated trying to sell to more technically oriented managers even when they had decision making authority. As a result, he was closing only 30% of the proposals he made and often failed to make his monthly quota.

Diagnosis: Mike was a driver type personality. As a buyer, he loved making quick decisions, was most interested in results and cared little about the process and the details. But the real problem was that Mike assumed that everyone bought the same way he did. As a result, he approached all his prospects from the same perspective. But, not everyone wanted to be sold the way Mike wanted to sell them.

Prescription: People are most comfortable dealing with people who approach life and business the same way they do (I like him; he's just like me). Personality differences can cause a sale to get sidetracked. In Mike's case, he failed to realize that he needed to adjust his approach with those buyers who were more analytical in nature. Analyticals represent about 15% of the population, but in Mike's case, because of the product he sold, analyticals represented about 30% of his potential buyers. So, in effect, he was unable to connect with nearly one third of his prospects because he failed to adjust his approach. He talked only about results when they wanted to know how those results would be achieved.

Don't make the same mistake Mike made. Not everyone buys the way you do. Determine if your buyer is a "driver", "socializer", "amiable" or "analytical" and adjust your approach accordingly. It's the fastest way we know to achieve a 15% sales increase.

Making The First
Ten Seconds Count

Problem: Stan always felt uncomfortable in those first few minutes when meeting prospects for the first time. He sensed that his prospects felt the same way when he met them. He wondered how his anxiousness affected his prospects and what impact it had on his sales calls and his income.

Diagnosis: You've heard this one a million times, but it's true. You have only 7-10 seconds when first meeting someone to make a favorable impression. People will form an impression of you when you first meet and anything less than perfect starts you out with one foot in the hole making it difficult to regain rapport and credibility. Statistics published by W. Brooks show that making an unfavorable first impression will reduce your chances of getting the business by 93%. Making a favorable impression is one of those areas of selling where a slight edge can make a huge difference.

Prescription: To refine and polish your first impression, there are several things to remember:

- Do your homework ahead of time and find out what your prospect's behavioral style is and, if appropriate, something about the person that you can ask about.
- Where appropriate, send a note or call in advance to confirm the appointment.
- Be on time.
- Dress properly for the occasion, but err on the side of being overdressed.

- Use their name when introduced. (A person's name is their most favorite word plus it will help you remember it later).
- Match their handshake and frequency of eye contact. Remember, body language is 55% of rapport.
- Be aware of appropriate distance, usually 4-5 feet for Drivers and Analytical styles, and 3-4 feet for Amiable and Socializer behavioral styles.
- Stand erect leaning in slightly. Too upright is often interpreted as confrontational and can be intimidating.
- Smile.

Draining The Pipeline
At Quarter's End

Problem: Steve called us the other day, frustrated with what he called the usual "end of the quarter scramble". In an effort to make their numbers at the end of every quarter, his reps were resorting more and more to pricing concessions to get business closed. What was worse, Steve felt that many of his company's customers had begun to expect these discounts and were waiting until the end of the quarter to place all but their most critical orders. In the last several quarters nearly 60% of their deals were closed in the last 10 days of the quarter and the trend was getting worse. The results were becoming disastrous to the bottom line and Steve usually had no idea of whether his group was going to make quota.

Diagnosis: Plain and simple, this is a qualifying issue. Steve's reps, lacking good qualifying skills, were resorting to giving discounts in order to overcome buyer hesitation. This causes a myriad of problems including, but not limited to, deteriorating margins, reduced commissions and bonuses, attitude problems within the sales force, turnover, and negative perceptions within the customer/prospect base.

Prescription: The ability to qualify prospects thoroughly is one of the most important skills salespeople can possess. Part of the qualifying process is to determine when the prospect needs to implement a solution and why it is important to implement the solution at that time. Without that information, the sales process can, and often will, continue indefinitely. Finding this sense of urgency is a function of developing the prospect's pain. There needs to be a real motivation to move forward quickly. Good questions that can help uncover this motivation are:

- "Is there a target date to get this done?"
- "What would happen if a solution was not implemented by the target date?"
- "Would there be a financial impact if the present situation were allowed to continue and, if so, how much?"
- "Would it be acceptable not to implement a solution by the target date?"
- "Assuming I was able to offer a solution that you felt would fix the problem, what would be the reasons not to implement it by the target date?"

If the prospect can't give you reasons why the deal shouldn't be done very quickly, he's probably not a very good prospect. If you ask the right questions, you can get the prospect to convince you that it's important to find a solution…now. And if you've asked the right questions and the answers indicate that there is no sense of urgency, find another prospect to help you make your quota at the end of the quarter.

How To Screw Up A Sure Thing

Problem: Tim, a software sales rep, had been having a rough day. He'd been bombarded with questions from several customers and had gotten behind on a proposal that he needed to finish before the end of the day. Then he got a call from Gene, a prospect who introduced himself by saying, "I've heard great things about your accounting software package. I saw a demo about a year ago, and was not in a position to purchase it at the time, but since then it's become very apparent that I need to integrate it immediately into my system."

"Wow", thought Tim. "This will be easy. It's about time something went right today."

Then Gene said, "I need to know about pricing and availability. And tech support is important, too. Tell me how that works."

Tim went into his pitch. He discussed tech support in detail, covered availability and other options, and explained that the price was $8000 with 30-day terms.

Gene's response was unexpected. He said that $8000 was quite a hefty price tag and he needed a couple of days to consider the purchase more carefully. He'd call Tim back next week.

Tim did a double take. "What just happened?" he thought. "This sale was in the bag, a sure thing, and now he's thinking it over? He said he needed the software right away." And that was the end of the call.

Diagnosis: Tim got lazy, plain and simple. He thought Gene was sold. All he had to do was give Gene the info he needed, then write it up. He got conned into doing a presentation without getting Gene to demonstrate why he was so excited about buying the software. The entire transaction was conducted at the intellectual level.

Prescription: Don't be lured into taking shortcuts. Don't mistake the prospect's enthusiasm for your product or service as a sure sale. Take the time to qualify the prospect and make sure he's real before you make your presentation. In Tim's case, a couple of quick questions would have made a world of difference. He might have said, "Before we discuss pricing, help me understand why this software is so important. I want to make sure the application is correct for you. Mind if I ask you a couple of questions?" Of course, you're probing for pain and one of the most important things to find out is the financial impact of not implementing a solution. Having discovered the financial impact and, assuming it was significant, you will find that the cost of the solution disappears as an objection.

Don't take shortcuts! Don't assume anything. Get the prospect involved at an emotional, not an intellectual, level. Use the system, qualify completely and get the sale.

Begin With The End In Mind

Problem: The biggest challenge salespeople face is closing more business. Typically, the problem is not the lack of closing skills per se, but rather the job they've done prior to the presentation and close. Would anyone disagree that the better the prospect is qualified, the easier the close will be?

Diagnosis: Old habits die hard. Most salespeople still can't wait to make a presentation, so they take short cuts qualifying. When a poor job has been done qualifying, we find that presentations are weak, causing a low closing rate. There is a direct relationship between qualifying and closing. The better the job salespeople do qualifying, the higher the closing rate will be. So, when closing rates are low, we have to find ways to qualify more effectively.

Prescription: Stephen Covey, in his great book, "The Seven Habits of Highly Effective People", suggests that we begin a project with the end in mind. It's good advice when you're trying to find the prospect's pain. Let's examine how this might work in selling.

Fast forward to your presentation. Let's pretend you had to give a presentation right now to a group of ten prospects from different companies who you had not had a chance to qualify beforehand. You don't know what their issues are. You'd have to tell them about every problem, need and want that your product or service addresses, wouldn't you? You couldn't leave anything out. You'd lead with your most important features and continue right down to your least important. You'd discuss each feature, its benefits and how it solves the problem. If you're like most salespeople, you can do that in your sleep. And, if you got a chance to do that, it would probably be an excellent presentation, at least to this group of people whose pains have yet to be determined.

However, not all the issues would be important for each person. Chances are there would be some commonality, but most would have their own unique set of challenges. Some of the information you presented would be irrelevant and your presentation would lose some of its effectiveness.

Make a list of the problems, needs and wants that your product or service addresses and use them as a checklist when you're qualifying. Your job then becomes one of asking questions to see which ones are important to the prospect and why. Then, when the time comes to make a presentation, your focus narrows only to those issues that are important to the prospect. Your presentation, therefore, is targeted and effective. Everything important is included and all irrelevant issues are omitted. That's a perfect presentation. Try it and watch your closing rate soar.

All's Well That Ends Well

Problem: Radio stations typically get "freebies" from local merchants in partial exchange for advertising time. These freebies are used for a variety of promotions and are an important way for radio stations to create interest in their stations. It seems KZAP had a few sets of tickets for a Shakespearean play at a local theater and decided to give them away. The DJ announced enthusiastically, "Okay folks, we've got great theater ticket this weekend at the Old Globe Theater for "All's Well That Ends Well", a Shakespearean classic. The fifth caller gets the tickets, so call 555-1234 right away. And they waited and waited, but the phone lines were silent. So they tried again the next hour with the same results. Two more efforts met with the same fate.

Diagnosis: Ho-hum. So what. Their listeners were tuned into a different station, WII-FM, What's In It For Me? Their offer failed to generate any enthusiasm in their listeners because they failed to give them an experience that they could relate to. OK, free tickets, but to Shakespeare? Not exactly everyone's choice for an exciting theater experience.

Prescription: At a meeting the following day, the general manager of the station recalled something he had read a few days before. People get excited about getting dressed up for a classy evening out. So they changed their pitch to the following, "If you'd like to have an evening out, want a reason to get dressed up and do something really classy, we've got just the ticket for you..... free tickets to see Shakespeare's 'All's Well That End's Well.' Tickets go to the fifth caller."

The phones lit up and the tickets were given away immediately. What was the difference? The audience was into the experience not the vehicle. The play was secondary. Think of the emotional value of getting dressed up for a night out doing something classy. It's light years ahead of simply attending a play by the Bard.

Are you getting your prospects involved emotionally or simply providing less than stimulating intellectual information?

Close The Sale <u>Before</u> You Present Solutions

Problem: Since closing rates are in the 15-20% range nationally, one of the biggest concerns that management and salespeople alike have is a desire to increase closing rates. Although there are several reasons for this problem, one of the most overlooked is the tendency for salespeople to make proposals without knowing what will happen when the prospect gets the proposal. This is like rolling the dice and hoping for the best.

Diagnosis: The traditional focus on closing has been to make sure we "ask for the business", memorize a few good "closes", or some other tactic. We've been told that we must qualify, make a presentation, and then close. We think that this approach makes little sense and puts the salesperson at a distinct disadvantage. Many salespeople don't want to appear pushy so they act subservient- they would rather make a friend than make a sale. If I ask for a commitment it will sound tricky, "salesy", and I might not like the answer. It's easy to see that old habits are hard to break.

Prescription: You have a right to get a commitment from your prospect before you "reward" them with a presentation. Think of it as trading a proposal for a decision.

Try saying something like this before you make the presentation: "Assuming you're totally convinced that our solutions will fix these problems for you, and the investment is within the parameters we've already discussed, what would happen at that point?" If you get a positive response, then all you've got to do is deliver. If you get something other than a positive response, chances are you have failed to qualify properly. If you don't like the prospect's answer, there's nothing in the rules that says you have to make a presentation.

Qualifying Proficiency
Determines Closing Efficiency

Problem: Salespeople spend far too much time preparing proposals and close far too few. Of course, closing rates vary, but closing only 15-20% of the proposals one makes is not uncommon. This is obviously very inefficient, causing time management problems, feelings of rejection, futility and despondence, not to mention reduced sales and lower commissions.

Diagnosis: Salespeople have been brainwashed over the years to believe that selling is a numbers game and that "if you throw enough stuff against the wall, some of it will stick". They believe that more is better and are eager to propose to virtually anyone who expresses even modest interest in their product or service. They delude themselves into thinking that business is good and that they are successful because there is a lot of activity going on. Well, the last time we checked, no one got paid commissions for doing proposals and the number of proposals on the street was not a line item on the company's P & L or Balance Sheet. Your banker probably won't give you a loan based on proposal activity.

Prescription: There's a direct relationship between the qualifying effort and the closing ratio. Studies show that in a complex sale the best investigators are the best closers. Never make a proposal unless you are confident that you've got at least a 90% chance of closing the deal. This requires you to do a world-class job of qualifying. Nothing less will do. You must have a clear understanding of exactly what problems or pains your prospect expects you to provide solutions to, understand completely how much they're willing to invest with you to fix the problems (assuming they're convinced your solutions are viable), and you must be talking with the decision maker. Finally, you must obtain a commitment from them before making the proposal. If you can manage to accomplish this, your closing rate will soar and so will your commissions.

Set The Trap... For Yourself!

Problem: Jack had been with the company for only two years, yet he was considered their most technically competent salesperson. He was the "go to guy" when the other salespeople needed someone to talk to about solutions, specifications, and competitive information. He was an expert when it came to product knowledge. Yet he had the worst closing rate and was the lowest paid salesperson.

Diagnosis: Jack had a bad habit and it was hurting his sales big time. He inevitably began to discuss solutions before he understood the prospect's problems. His product knowledge and technical expertise was causing failure, not success. Despite the training he'd had over the years that taught him to diagnose the prospect's problem before prescribing a solution, it seemed he just couldn't help himself. He <u>had</u> to talk about his product. Deep down he believed that when they heard about all the features, advantages and benefits, they'd be compelled to buy. And he believed that dispensing his solutions and other free advice would endear him to his prospects. But it didn't! He had to do something or he'd be looking for another job. What a waste of good product knowledge that would be!

Prescription: Jack came to us for advice. He understood the problem, but seemed helpless to break the habit after several months of trying. We suggested that he "set a trap" for himself. We told him to tell every prospect during the meeting agreement, "You know, one of the biggest concerns I have is that I get so excited about our products that I often start selling them before I've taken the time to really understand what the customer needs. It's not very fair to you, so if I start to do this today, will you please stop me? After all, I can't be much help to you if I don't understand your issues, can I?"

Now, not many prospects would actually stop him in the middle of his sales pitch, but it gave him an excuse to stop himself! He learned to say, "I'm sorry, there I go again. I told you I might do too much talking. Can we go back a step? I'd like to ask you a question about...." This "trap" helped him eliminate premature product knowledge dumping, got him to ask more questions, qualify better, and build better rapport because his prospects felt he really cared about their issue. Best of all, he closed more business.

What bad selling habits do you have? Do you forget to discuss money issues, fail to get to the real decision maker, never get referrals? How can you use a "trap" to help you?

The Qualification Trifecta

Problem: Gerry was fortunate. His company's new marketing program resulted in a great deal of incoming calls. Daily he received at least 2-3 calls from interested prospects who wanted to see him. It was a salesperson's dream. No more cold calls and lots of appointments. But at the end of the quarter, his sales had not increased. In fact, his closing rate had declined to 15%. What happened?

Diagnosis: Prospects are motivated by a number of things and it's critical to understand the motivational hierarchy of pain, fear and interest. Pain is a problem today, fear is concern about future pain, and interest is often nothing more than simple curiosity. People spend the most to fix pain, and the least on interest. Gerry was often mistaking interest for pain.

Let's take a moment to understand these concepts better. People will spend a lot of money to eliminate pain, especially if the pain has serious financial implications, and they'll spend it now. Fear is compelling as well, although generally less compelling than pain. Because it's not as urgent, they're likely to allocate less funds and will postpone the purchase for a short period of time, depending on the imminence of the problem they're worried about. Interest, on the other hand, is by far the least compelling. People will spend very little on "interest" and making an investment quickly is likely only if the cost is minimal. It is, however, important to note that many purchases seem to begin with nothing more compelling than a mild interest in the product or service. The skilled salesperson, by asking questions, is often able to uncover the true motivations which, in some cases, may not be that apparent to the prospect. Thus, the salesperson can play an important role in helping the prospect elevate the motivation from interest to fear and, perhaps, to pain.

Prescription: Sometimes the most important qualifying questions are the ones you ask yourself. Do you really know the prospect's level of motivation? Are you mistaking "interest" for "pain"? If you're not sure, try asking yourself the following questions as you interview the prospect: "What am I dealing with here? Does the prospect have a problem that she is committing to fix now or is she just worried that if she doesn't start to address some issues she'll have a problem later? When is later? Or, is the prospect simply fishing for information?" If you can't answer those questions, you haven't done a very good job qualifying the prospect. Keep working the qualification process until you're positive which of the qualification trifecta (pain, fear or interest) you're dealing with. Then you can decide how much time to invest with the prospect.

Eliminate Mutual Confusion

Problem: Ever go on a sales call where there seemed to be little structure, where both parties seemed to be on different pages, where expectations were not met, and little was accomplished? Even worse, you expected something positive to occur but simply got a luke warm response such as, "I need to think it over. Call me in a few days." Opportunities are squandered and the buyer seems to be in control.

Diagnosis: All too often sales calls are unstructured; objectives are not determined or communicated. Winging it seems to be the primary strategy employed by the salesperson. Assumptions are made that the buyer knows why you're there and no clarification of purpose is needed.

Prescription: The key to successfully implementing the Common Sense Selling approach and taking the lead in the selling interview is to agree early in the meeting as to exactly what the agenda will be. You must determine with your prospect the amount of time available for the meeting, what the prospect would like to accomplish for it to be a successful meeting, obtain permission to ask questions to get a better understanding of the prospect's needs, and agree that at the end of the meeting, at the very least, you'll make a decision as to whether or not to continue talking.

If you have a very clear meeting agreement, you'll build tremendous rapport with the prospect, improve communication significantly because both parties have the opportunity to ask questions, eliminate premature presentations, get decisions and eliminate "think it overs" and, most importantly, take leadership of the selling interview. In addition, our clients tell us that prospects visibly begin to relax when they hear that the seller is comfortable with hearing "no". The meeting agreement is one of the most effective selling tools you'll ever own...master it and you're well on your way to becoming a true sales superstar.

"We'd Like To See A Demo"

Problem: Technology companies place a great deal of reliance on demos to showcase their products and services. While a demo is a great way to show off your product, it is not being properly utilized to close business. Salespeople arrive, anxious to show how their product will improve the prospect's situation. They demo every feature and discuss every benefit. Typically when the demo is finished, the prospect expresses their interest and says they need some time to think it over and invite the salesperson to follow up in a week or two. Whatever the final result, too little business seems to be closed as a result of the demo.

Diagnosis: It's yet another case of the buyer using his system successfully. They get the salesperson to cough up his information (the product demo) early in the cycle, carefully avoid making a commitment when the demo is concluded, and force the salesperson to invest considerable time following up. Unfortunately, companies believe that if the prospect would just take the time to see how the product works, they'd recognize the benefits and buy. Too bad that doesn't happen as often as it should. The real problem lies not with the demo itself, but with the way the salesperson deals with the opportunity.

Prescription: A prospect that asks for or agrees to a demo is not necessarily a qualified prospect. Take the time to find out not only what the issues are, but also their budget and decision making process. And when you do agree to do a demo, make sure you've asked these three questions beforehand:
- "What issues do you want the demo to address?"
- "How will you determine if they were addressed successfully?"

- "Assuming we are able to address your issues successfully, what would happen at the end of the demo?"

By getting answers to these questions you'll be able to accomplish several very important things. First, you can focus the demo on the prospect's pain and avoid showing other features that may not be relevant. Second, you'll get an understanding of how your demo will be measured and you'll have the right to ask whether or not you were successful. Finally, you'll know what the next step should be after the demo and avoid the ubiquitous "I need to think it over". In fact, you may even get an order.

Good Cop, Bad Cop

Problem: Casey had made a presentation to a large shipyard that had been awarded the contract to build one of the Navy's newest amphibious ships.   This was an important deal for his company, a seven-figure sale over the next two years.   Casey knew that he was the front-runner and, if the company did not accept his proposal, another six months would be wasted because the engineering drawings would have to be revised. He knew that this presented an unacceptable situation for the shipyard.   Nevertheless, the buyer was stalling him on making a decision. Casey had tried everything to get them to make a move, but to no avail.   And to make matters worse, he was getting the feeling that if he continued to be assertive in soliciting a decision, he might hurt the rapport that he'd worked so hard to establish. Have you ever been in this position?

Diagnosis: Why decisions aren't made more quickly is anybody's guess. The circumstances can certainly vary in every situation. This much is known: buyers have their own timetable and it isn't always in sync with the seller's. Perhaps the buyer had misled Casey about when a decision would be made or maybe some internal issues had delayed their ability to make a decision. But in this case, Casey felt his buyer was simply playing games.

Prescription: Casey went to the buyer and said the following: "Paul, I've got a problem and I need your help. As you know, you and I have worked very hard on this proposal over the last six months. But for whatever reason, we're apparently not close to getting a decision.   I'm getting an unbelievable amount of pressure from my company president to get this deal closed. In fact, he said that I can't afford to spend any more time on this project and has asked me to pull the proposal off the table if we can't get a decision in a week. I don't know what problems that might cause for you, but I thought you should know my limitations."

Sound familiar? It's a tactic used by police when they're interrogating a suspect. "Good cop, bad cop" is an effective way to raise an unpleasant issue without hurting rapport between you and your prospect. Casey got his buyer to move.

Can you think of any situations when you could use "good cop, bad cop"?

Easy Exits

Problem: Salespeople are so predictable! They use the "pull" approach, constantly trying to convince and persuade their prospects to buy from them. Of course, their prospects are on to these tactics and are doing their best to "push" the salesperson away. Often, even good prospects feel trapped and push the salesperson away because they don't want to be sold.

Diagnosis: Clearly a new approach is needed. Why not try the push approach when selling, from time to time? Giving the prospect an easy exit, pushing them away, can have magical results when you have a good prospect.

Prescription: An "easy exit" is an opportunity for you to make the prospect feel comfortable by bringing up situations that may still be a source of concern and let the prospect deal with them. In effect, you're providing them with an "easy exit". You'll find that one of two things will happen: they'll convince you that your concern is unwarranted and that it's really not an issue (proving to you that they really are a good prospect) or they'll admit that your concern is valid. This gives you a chance to probe for more pain or to take it to "no", thus arriving at the right conclusion for both parties without wasting everyone's time. In either case, rapport is maintained, even strengthened, and you're doing the disqualifying, not them. Here are a few examples:

During your initial meeting say, "If we don't have a fit, it's okay to tell me."
> *or*

"We may spend some time together today looking at your situation only to find that we're not the right solution for you. If we're not, you need to be comfortable telling me that. Okay?"

When the prospect begins to discuss his challenges say, "That problem doesn't sound like it's causing you that much trouble. Are you sure it's really that important to fix?"

or

"It doesn't appear that the company is really that committed to finding a solution now. Wouldn't you agree?"

During your budget discussion try, "I get the feeling that this is much more than you had planned to spend. Do we need to talk further about that?"

You need to keep your "antenna" up at all times to assess what the prospects are implying when they make a statement. Often a prospect will not tell you the whole truth regarding a problem, but will send out bits of (mis)information instead. It's your job to relieve pressure and help discover what the prospect is really saying (see the above examples). Your role is to gently minimize the prospect's assertions of pain and their commitment to do something to fix it, thus getting them to defend their position and prove to you that they are a good prospect with real pain and a real commitment to finding a solution. Any time you give them a chance to run away from doing business with you and they don't take that chance, they're sending a message that they want to do business.

Don't Get Stuck In The Middle

Problem: Meagan came back from a sales call and told me a story that I have heard many times before. She said that the sales interview went well. She had good rapport and the prospect liked her. The prospect said he would call her next week to give her a decision on whether he wanted a proposal as soon as he gets back from a company meeting. Meagan really wanted to believe that her prospect would call her back but her "gut" told her that a return call was unlikely.

Diagnosis: Two major faults could be the source of this problem: first is not knowing what a <u>genuine</u> commitment from a prospect sounds like; and, second is being afraid to ask for it. Salespeople are often overly cautious after a first interview and hesitate to press for a commitment of some kind from a prospect. This is especially true when they have good rapport and they do not want to risk destroying it by being "pushy". It is far more comfortable to be optimistic and believe that a prospect is more interested than they really are.

Prescription: First, early in the meeting obtain agreement that there will be a clear outcome by the end of the meeting. The prospect must realize that it is acceptable to tell you that they do not see a fit between what you are selling and their situation. When a prospect feels that "no" is an acceptable response, they will be less likely to feel pressure to feign some sort of commitment to get rid of you at the end of the meeting. This may not completely eliminate the problem because prospects are not used to dealing with salespeople who will accept "no" as a response. You will know a genuine commitment when you hear it because it includes a specific action to be completed by a certain date leading toward the decision to be made.

When faced with a prospect who does not indicate commitment near the end of an interaction, an effective step toward determining their intent is to take a fall back position and ask a negative question. You will not be perceived as "pushy" if you say something like, "My sense is that you have doubts about whether we should move forward. Would you agree?" or "I get the feeling that this is really a low priority for you and you don't know how to tell me that. If you don't see a fit, I'll understand, okay?" When using this approach the prospect will either agree with you (it may be over) or move in a positive direction (they will convince you of their commitment) and you will avoid getting stuck in the middle.

Break The Rules And Win More Bids

Problem: Many companies are frustrated because they have to participate in a competitive bidding process to obtain business. Winning is often based on having the lowest bid. More than in any other type of sale, the buyer is in total control of the process. All information is disseminated to the bidders at a common bid conference and individual meetings are rare. The seller has no advantage over his competitors and frequently is reduced to guessing what his company will need to win the bid. If there are six qualified companies bidding, your chances are less than 20% of winning the bid. And if you're the "lucky" one that is awarded the bid, chances are your margins won't be as healthy as you'd like.

Diagnosis: Typically, prospects use the bidding process to avoid having to deal with salespeople. But for the salesperson, failure to have access to the buyer is a recipe for disaster. You must find a way to take control from the buyer if you are to improve both your chances of being awarded the bid and arrange to generate higher profit margins on the contract. In other words, submit the bid on your terms, not the buyer's. To do this, we suggest the following "re-direct" strategy.

Prescription: Get the buyer aside and say the following, "We've looked at the bid specs and see some problems. It looks like you might have made some mistakes in planning. If we bid the contract the way it's set up, you're going to have problems. By the way, have you ever awarded a contract only to discover that there are cost overruns, lots of change orders, and the work not done on time? That's probably because the specs were flawed from the beginning." (Most contracts have cost overruns, changes orders, etc. because the specs are often flawed, so the buyer can always relate to that.)

Continue with this tactic to take control of the bid process. "If you want us to bid, here's what we suggest...let us come in and review the bid specs. We'll have to charge for this service, but you'll get it back if we are awarded the bid. I've got to tell you one thing, we're higher but you'll make up for that during the course of the contract since there'll be less cost overruns, etc."

Sell the analysis, re-write the specs to favor your company and enjoy a much higher close rate and higher margins.

The Gridlocked Prospect

Problem: You're in that familiar, albeit uncomfortable, position of having to chase a prospect who told you they were interested. But, based on their failure to commit, it appears that they are not. Initially, they seemed very convincing in their interest regarding your product or service (as they nearly always are). Since then your tactic has been to try to get their ear so that you can tell your story more convincingly, provide a comprehensive review of your features and benefits, and ferret out any objections that might be blocking the sale. To that end you've been persistent, called them at least weekly, sometimes more. But that has yielded no tangible results and now you're fearful that you're becoming a pest.

Diagnosis: You believed all the positive things they told you in your initial conversation. You may have even included them in your sales forecast. You exhibited the typical trust and optimism that characterize most salespeople. Now you're playing hide and seek with the prospect and losing. Worst of all, you failed to agree with them about what your next step would be. So, now you're stuck.

Prescription: Traditionalists beware! This is a tough one for many salespeople, but it's the only way you'll be able to regain control. However, you'll have to overcome all your old instincts to continue to sell. This may take some doing since you will want to think you've still got a chance. But, you have to call the game! Take it to "no"! Change your assumption from the answer being a "yes" to it being a "no" and tell them.

Find a way to get through to the "prospect" and explain that you haven't been reading the signals very well and, based on his failure to return your calls, you believe that they have no interest in moving forward so you're going to close the file. If they are still interested, they'll tell you. If not, you've just liberated yourself from another wild goose chase.

Sleepless In San Diego

Problem: Marcia was a successful life insurance agent, but she suffered from insomnia every time she made a sale. When we asked why, she replied that about 40% of the time, when she closed a deal, the new "client" would call her the next day (but usually not during working hours) and leave a voice mail backing out of the deal. Typically, they would say that they had had second thoughts and decided, after all, that they really didn't need the policy.

Diagnosis: Marcia's prospects were experiencing a predictable psychological aftereffect in the selling process known as "buyer's remorse". Marcia had been trained in her industry to build rapport at the beginning of the call and she was very good at it. She was also trained that when she got the order, she was supposed to complete the paperwork, get the check and get out. The theory was that if you stayed, the buyer might have second thoughts and you would lose the sale. Typically, the prospect felt that her quick exit sent the message that "I'd better get out of here before they change their minds". Combined with some unresolved concerns, prospects became uncomfortable enough to back out the next day. Unfortunately, Marcia was able to resurrect very few of these back-outs.

Prescription: Regardless of the product or service that you're selling, give the buyer a parachute. Give them a chance to back out. Buyer's remorse can be a real issue and is very predictable even if you haven't resorted to manipulation to get the sale. Giving the buyer a chance to back out, although considered selling heresy by most traditionalists, will give you an opportunity to save the sale when there is buyer's remorse. Try saying something like this: "I really appreciate your business and look forward to working with you. Before I leave, however, I just want to make sure you're comfortable with what we've discussed. If there's anything that you're not sure about, this would be a good time to discuss it." Usually about 90% of the time the buyer will reinforce her decision to do business with you. If she does bring up an issue, you will be there to deal with it.

The Hammer Isn't Always The Right Tool

Problem: Mark was a high tech salesperson, selling complex hardware and software solutions to distribution companies. Relatively new to the job, his ability to close was frustratingly poor. But he was in good company, as the other salespeople in the company suffered from the same problem.

Diagnosis: Bernie was Mark's sales manager, and was "old school". He was a disciple of J. Douglas Edwards who, along with Dale Carnegie, is considered the father of sales training. Bernie has been in sales for 30 years and had learned his craft well. He was proud of the fact that he had been successful selling a variety of products, starting with vacuum cleaners and progressing to aluminum siding, and then retail computer parts before landing a job with a harddrive manufacturer. Recently, he convinced the president of this company to hire him to manage the sales effort. He loved to regale his troops about his closing prowess, telling them that the best salespeople were the ones who could sell something to someone who didn't need it. Of course, his techniques were highly manipulative and they worked in those selling situations where he had experience. He subscribed to many sales technique magazines and required his people to memorize the closes. The sales trainers he hired to train his people reinforced these manipulative techniques. "Tell them our story and then go for the close", exhorted Bernie as he rehearsed his people in selling features and benefits. Of course, Bernie *was* the problem.

Prescription: Bernie, like too many other sales managers, failed to realize that there's a big difference between the simple sale (vacuums, siding and other "commodity" type products) and the complex sale. A short selling cycle where quick decisions are made primarily on price characterizes the simple sale. It's basically a transaction. The consumer knows the product well and is mostly concerned with price and availability. The salesperson brings little to the relationship, except the ability to agree to a lower price in order to get the order. The problem was that Bernie's company sold complex solutions to a sophisticated customer. The complex sale is characterized by a longer selling cycle, multiple decision makers and influencers, a relatively large financial investment, and a high degree of risk for the buyer if a wrong decision is made. In a complex sale, the relationship between buyer and seller is key because it's typically not a one shot deal; the seller will be involved well past the contract signing. For that reason, manipulative techniques simply turn off the buyer.

The complex sale must be consultative. The seller must be able to understand the buyer's issues and then prescribe a solution. When a seller can do this, he brings value to the relationship. If you're in a complex sale business and you treat the sale as a transaction, you'll never reach your true potential.

Try A Pattern Interrupt For Better Sales Results

Problem: Kim, a ten-year sales veteran, never felt like she was in control of her sales calls. She felt like her prospects and customers were always one step ahead of her. She attended many training sessions and they all basically taught her the same thing: always ask for the order, use the same 2-3 foolproof ways to overcome the price objection, lead with, "If I could show you a way to fix that problem, would you buy my product?" She felt these tactics must be effective since all the trainers taught the same approaches. Why weren't they working for her?

Diagnosis: Salespeople tend to be rather predictable and, as a result, buyers generally are in charge. They recognize the salesperson's approaches and have developed effective ways to deal with those approaches. To illustrate this point, have you ever been doing something on "autopilot" such as driving a car? You get too close to the car in front and you apply the brakes. In a dangerous situation you honk the horn to warn another driver. Neither activity requires you to stop and think. You're definitely not saying to yourself, "What should I do here? Oh yeah, let's honk the horn, that's a good idea." By then it's too late anyway. You just do it. That's autopilot. That's how we react instinctively to a situation. Dealing with salespeople is a familiar situation to everyone and we all go on autopilot when we're face to face with a salesperson. In effect, salespeople build their own roadblocks by being so predictable.

Prescription: Don't act like the typical salesperson. Do the unexpected. Try a "pattern interrupt" and keep your prospect off autopilot. Here are a few examples:

- Ask, "Sounds like I caught you at a bad time?" when you connect by phone.
- Let your prospect know, "It's okay to say "no" if we don't have a fit".
- Don't jump on every "buying signal" you hear and try to close.   Instead, use a well-placed easy exit or takeaway to get the prospect to sell himself, "Really, I had no idea the impact was that significant."
- Do your best Colombo routine, "I'm kind of confused, can you help me understand why that's so important to the company?"

You get the idea. Be different. Your sales results will be different, too. They'll be better.

Wimping Out

Problem: As trainers, we see this scenario played out time and time again. Salespeople seem to have lost the ability to close!

Diagnosis: Selling, from a technical/skill perspective, has gone through a major transition. Years ago, salespeople were taught what we might call the *CHAOS* System of Selling, Close Hard And Often System. Pound away until you get the order, be extremely persistent, manipulate if necessary, and use one of the many canned closes that worked so well back in the 1950's. ("If I could show you a way, would you buy it today?" is a typical example of the worst in sales approaches.)

The buying public caught on, became much more aware of the sales technique, and quickly learned how to deal with obvious manipulative approaches. Salespeople, who are also buyers, learned to hate these approaches as well. So, except for a few diehards, salespeople backed-off using many of the old techniques. Sales processes were adapted to take on a more laid back "consultative" approach, at least early in the process. Yet often these consultative approaches concluded with some sort of old style manipulative closes.

When almost everyone realized that manipulation was no longer effective, a 180-degree turn for the worse occurred. Many salespeople stopped trying to close at all. (Witness the often stated complaint of sales managers, "nobody asks for the order.") Buyers started to "think it over" more often, the sales cycle got longer and everyone, except the buyer got frustrated. Salespeople made lots of friends, but business was still in the tank. Plain and simple, salespeople were "wimping out"!

Prescription: The old selling model is clearly flawed and a new paradigm is needed. The new model is for salespeople to facilitate the buying process. The idea is to let the buyer convince you, the salesperson, that he really needs your product or service. It takes a good meeting agreement, strong qualifying skills, and the ability (and guts) to recognize when someone is not a prospect. Master these skills, change your attitude about hearing "no", and you'll be selling more with less effort.

When All Else Fails, Become A Consultant

Problem: Have you ever run into a prospect who just doesn't "get it"? You've done your job well. They've convinced you they have a problem that they really want to fix, you've determined that you're in front of the person who can make the decision, and found out that they have the financial resources to fix the problem. You've presented a solution that works perfectly and satisfies all the issues that they expressed. But, in spite of all that, they have decided to go with a competitor who has a less effective solution, perhaps one that really is a bad choice for them. Every bone in your body wants to tell them that they are screwing up, but you just don't know how to say it? So you walk away confused and dejected.

Diagnosis: Sometimes prospects may be confused about how to make a selection or may have been promised some unrealistic things by a competitor. Whatever the reason, they don't always make the right decisions.

Prescription: When you know with 100% conviction that the prospect is making a real mistake, you owe it to them to be honest and tell them. But to do it graciously without coming across as a rejected suitor is difficult. Here's a way to pull it off, but remember, you're no longer selling. You are, instead, becoming a consultant. Simply say this, "Mr. Prospect, I understand and respect your decision to use my competiton, and I'm through selling, so can I tell you something without you getting mad at me?" Typically they'll give you permission. Continue by saying, "I'm no longer selling, so can I offer some advice? (Pause) You're making a big mistake. With all due respect to my competition, the solution you've chosen is flawed. Here's why."

This tactic is not to be used to vent your frustrations when you've been outsold, only when the prospect is making a mistake and you can substantiate that fact. The key here is to acknowledge that you're no longer in a sales mode. The competition has won and you're simply acting as consultant who has their permission to offer advice. After all, consultants point out problems and suggest solutions. It's a last ditch effort that sometimes pays dividends.

Too Many Options

Problem: Jason, a home remodeling salesperson, was frustrated by his prospect's unwillingness to make a decision. He had qualified extensively and had made exactly the presentation that the prospect wanted. The prospect had stated several times that he really needed to get the remodel done quickly. He really felt that this one was "in the bag" and he'd leave with an order. But that didn't happen. Instead, Jason's prospect said he needed some time to digest the proposal before making a decision. He added that he was pleased with the proposal and that Jason had obviously done his job well. Now Jason found himself in the "chase" mode because the prospect wasn't returning his calls.

Diagnosis: The prospect had asked Jason to provide him with three options to choose from: the first was the low priced economy program; the second the standard version which was the prospect's initial preference; and the third was the "Rolls Royce" version which the prospect said he could afford. The first and third options seemed to be almost an afterthought, having been requested just before Jason left. With three options to consider, it was necessary for the prospect to do an "analysis" of the options. This analysis became an intellectual activity, weighing the pros and cons and checking the cost/benefit ratios which led the buyer to wonder if he needed more information and whether he had the best price. He began to think about checking with other vendors and the entire buying process broke down. Lost in this intellectual activity was the emotional reason why he wanted to make the purchase in the first place.

Prescription: People buy emotionally, and simply justify their purchasing decisions intellectually. Jason, in his

136

attempt to be responsive to the prospect, had lost the emotional leverage that he initially had. He gave his prospect too much to think about. Jason should have qualified further when the prospect asked for additional options. He should have discovered why the prospect was asking for other options and discussed them thoroughly enough to eliminate all but one. Then he could have easily gotten a "yes" or "no" when he made his proposal.

The bottom line is...don't give your prospects too many options, qualify more effectively and stay in control of the process.

Show Me The Money

Problem: Why is money so difficult to discuss? Salespeople frequently hear from prospects that budget is "no problem" at the beginning of the sales call. However, once things start to get close, the story sometimes changes. We're told that we "have to sharpen our pencil", "get more competitive" or offer "additional discounts". And yet, once the sale is won, price seems to evaporate as an issue and pressure is put on the vendor to improve quality or service. Often we hear from salespeople that money is the number one issue in getting and keeping the business. We need to have more competitive pricing, better discount structures or we just can't compete. You've heard it all before.

Diagnosis: There are several reasons that investment or budget is discussed only superficially. First, is the unfortunate, self-limiting belief (that afflicts many, but not all salespeople) that discussing financial issues is impolite. Second, experience has shown us that a discussion of price typically deteriorates into a negotiation situation which is uncomfortable. Third, we're afraid that the prospect may not be able to afford our product. Fourth, deep down, we may not be convinced that our product is really worth what we're asking.

Prescription: Don't ever get yourself into a situation where you're making a proposal without finding out two things: 1) how much the problem is costing the prospect, and 2) how much they'd be willing to spend assuming your solution completely fixed the problem. It's imperative that you understand all the financial parameters related to the sale. One effective way to make sure budget and related money issues are discussed is for you to set a "trap" for yourself. It goes something like this: "Mr. Prospect, one of the things that I sometimes find difficult to discuss is budgetary issues related to purchasing my product. I'm not sure why that is, but I want to make sure that we take some time to talk about that today. Is that okay with you?" This "trap" lets the prospect know up-front that money issues will be part of the discussion and gives you an excuse to bring them up. You might say, "Do you remember that we wanted to discuss your budget for this type of purchase? Can we do that now?"

Oh, yeah! One last thing -- don't spend your valuable selling time with someone who doesn't have the financial resources to buy your product or service.

"We're Thinking About Making A Change"

Problem: How gullible we salespeople are! Steve had heard it all before, but every time he heard prospects say they were thinking about changing suppliers or that they had heard good things about his company, Steve breathed a sigh of relief. He wanted to believe that this one would be easier, that this one might be the lay down that he needed to give him a respite from the highly competitive selling environment he found himself in. So when Apex Circuits, one of his top prospects, called and said they were thinking about firing his major competitor, Steve took the bait. But three months later, his competitor still had the business and Steve couldn't get Apex to return his calls. Bummer, big time.

Diagnosis: Prospects set traps for salespeople. They know how to get you to do a little consulting (unpaid, of course) for them. It sounds like this: "How would you go about solving this problem?" "We've heard good things about your company." We're not so happy with our current supplier and might be making a change soon." And salespeople, not wanting to rock the boat by asking too many questions, take the bait, hook, line and sinker. Let's face it, like everyone else, salespeople are looking for the path of least resistance so we play into the prospect's hands. Our optimistic nature pretty much takes over. We just can't help ourselves. The slippery slide into unpaid consulting begins.

Prescription: You can be optimistic about your career, but be pessimistic about what your prospects tell you. After all, they've got a system that gets them great results when dealing with salespeople. They know how to get you to spend lots of time putting together a detailed proposal that is often used to negotiate a better deal with their current supplier. Don't take the bait. Ask the hard questions and get answers to the things you need to know. Here are a few good questions to ask:

- "Why would you be thinking about a change? So and so is a good supplier."
- "I can't believe the problem is severe enough for you to consider a supplier change."
- "If we were able to find solutions to those challenges, would you seriously consider changing suppliers?"

What would the answers tell you? Plenty, to be sure. You'd find out in a hurry whether or not you have a good prospect. The bottom line is that a little skepticism can go a long way when dealing with a seemingly positive prospect. Get them to do a little selling for you. Don't fall for the trap. Make them convince you that they're for real!

The Bag Dive

Problem: Recently I was speaking with Fred, a salesperson who told a story that I could well relate to. He was lamenting that on his last trip to New York to meet with some prospects for the first time, the airline lost his luggage. Now we all know what a pain that can be, but Fred was mostly concerned that his big black bag containing all his collateral sales material had been lost. Quite frankly, he was uncomfortable on a sales call without it. After all, he was accustomed to doing the "bag dive" when the prospect baited him with this innocent, yet misleading question, "tell me about your company." Of course, the "bag dive" was the move he made toward his briefcase to haul out the company and product brochures when this request was made. Fred figured that this was a good thing since the company had invested heavily in lots of sales collateral for him and the rest of the sales department so they could tell their story. Marketing departments like to do this.

Diagnosis: Salespeople rely far too heavily on their literature. The moment the prospect asks them a question about their company or products and they have some slick glossies to help them with the answer, the long slow slide to "unpaid consulting" has begun.

Prescription: The answer is quite simple. Don't take any literature with you, none, nada. If that makes you just a little bit uncomfortable, it's understandable. But it's quite easy to say early on in the conversation, "You know, I didn't bring literature with me today. I wasn't sure what to bring since I really don't have a good understanding of your issues. Maybe we could spend some time just talking about what you're looking for. Does that make sense?"

Typically the prospect sees this as his invitation to start discussing his issues.

Remember, the moment you start diving into the bag and breaking out the brochures, your presentation has begun; the info dump has started. After that, it's too late to go back and start qualifying. They have your information. The only thing left to do is ask for the business. When you've failed to qualify thoroughly, your chances of getting the business are poor. So, leave the literature at home and learn how to ask questions instead.

White Knights & Black Knights

Problem: Sean was frustrated. Twice in one month he had been sabotaged by someone in the prospect's organization after he thought he had made a sale. In both situations he'd been in front of the decision maker, but both sales fell through nevertheless. Ever happen to you?

Diagnosis: Sean had done a great job of getting in front of the decision maker, but he had failed to determine if there were any influencers who might favor another vendor. Let's face it, often others in the company are able to get Vito's ear and persuade him that your solution might not be the best. These people are called the "black knights" because they favor your competition or, even worse, have developed a bias against you, your company or your product.

Prescription: While we preach that you must be in front of the decision maker, you cannot overlook the influencers. You may have a number of people who favor your solution, obviously they're your "white knights", but one black knight can ruin the whole party. Authority is found in the organizational chart, while influence is found behind the scenes. An important part of your strategy should be to discover who the black knights are and enlist the assistance of your white knights in neutralizing their negative influence. Take a moment to ask your supporters, "Who in the organization might not want to see us get the business and why? How can you help me make sure they don't sabotage our efforts?" Obviously, this tactic requires that you have very strong support from your white knights but, after all, isn't that what selling is all about?

The Brochure Brush-Off

Problem: We often hear from our clients that when they finally get past the secretary, the prospect requests literature prior to committing to see them…and after the literature has been sent, they can't get the prospect back on the phone.

Everyone who is selling anything has been there over and over. Salespeople have tons of literature from the marketing department to mail to prospects who request information. The problem is that 99% of the literature that is sent out becomes just "litter". A bigger problem is that the salesperson is under the illusion that the prospect is really interested and will give them an appointment. The reality is that they were relegated to the trash heap with the proven "Send me a brochure brush-off".

Diagnosis: Most salespeople think anything other than a "no" keeps them in the game. They mistakenly look at a "no" as a failure on their part. Many salespeople actually believe their prospects need to see literature prior to an appointment.

Prescription: Track your sales history. How many sales were made when the *first step* in the process was to send a brochure? If your experience is similar to people we talk to, the number is painfully low. The only people who benefit from the sending of literature are your printer, the postal service, and your competitor as it will probably end up with them or with the trash hauler.

You are in total control of whether or not to <u>agree</u> to send literature. You should not send literature unless you understand what the prospect wants to know and exactly what is going to happen after the prospect has it. The only way to know for sure is to ask questions until you hear the answers you need to hear. If you have been able to keep the prospect speaking long enough to find these things out, you should be able to get an appointment to see him. But, if you can't, and you absolutely must send information, send only the information that relates to the prospect's pain - nothing else. Too much information may get you disqualified or cause the prospect to procrastinate about reading it. Then set a strong meeting agreement for your next step. Ask how long they will need to read it. Agree on a date and time to call them to see whether it makes sense to meet or close the file.

Unless you have a good understanding of your prospects' pain and a firm commitment from the prospect to do something once they have the literature, don't waste your time or the company's money.

High Tech Trade Show "Selling"

Problem: Companies invest many thousands of dollars attending trade shows annually. Often the results are disappointing. When asked why they continue to attend, we hear things like, "if we don't attend our customers will think we're in trouble" and "our competitors are there, so we need to be." Hardly an offensive strategy, wouldn't you agree? If you're wondering why the results aren't so hot, at least part of the answer lies in this story.

Diagnosis: A close friend of ours attended a high tech trade show recently. He's semi-retired and was there primarily because he was thinking about developing content for a computer based training program and wanted to see what the latest and greatest was in streaming media technology. He reported the following back to us:

"I was somewhat apprehensive about attending this show since I'm not a very technically oriented person. I was interested to see what was out there in the way of streaming media that I might utilize for a program that I was thinking about creating. After I stopped at the first booth that looked interesting, my worst fears were realized. I asked a fellow named Chuck, the west coast regional sales manager, what his company did as it was the only question I could think to ask without exposing my ignorance. He immediately took me to a PC and launched into a demo of the software and hardware his company offered. Of course, I asked very few questions which seemed only to encourage Chuck to show me more features of the product. I assume he was trying to find something that I'd get excited about. After about 10 minutes he asked me if I had any questions. The only one I could think to ask was whether or not he had a brochure I could take with me. It was the only way I could think of to get out of there.

After I left Chuck's booth it occurred to me that he had never once asked me any questions about what I did, what I was looking for or why I had stopped by his booth. I was not a prospect for him and yet he had invested considerable time with me without ever finding this out. It was unbelievable. How much sense does that make? I couldn't help wondering how many people who might have been good prospects walked by the booth without stopping because Chuck and his associates were busy talking to non-prospects like myself."

Our friend went on to say that his experience at this booth was hardly unusual. In fact, it was the norm. Nobody asked any questions, preferring instead to provide comprehensive technical demonstrations of their products and services.

Prescription: No wonder so many of these high tech companies are in trouble. Their "salespeople" are confused about what selling really is. A demo to anybody before you've qualified them is not selling. Quite the contrary, it could be self-sabotage. Qualify first.

Try asking these simple questions at your next trade show before you get the urge to do a demo:

- "What do you do?"
- "What prompted you to stop by our booth?"
- "What challenges are you looking to resolve at this show?"

These two questions should give you enough information to decide whether or not to spend more time with the suspect and what questions to ask next to qualify more extensively.

Column Filler

Problem: Lisa was angry. It had happened too many times. She recalled the old movie, "Network", where the veteran news anchor said, "I'm mad as hell and I won't take it any more!"

After submitting yet another proposal, she determined that she was just one of several vendors who were being used to satisfy the prospect's need to obtain competitive bids. They had already selected a vendor (often the incumbent), and Lisa's numbers were just needed to fill in column B or C. That way the prospect could say that they had gotten several competitive bids. So that's exactly how Lisa felt..."mad as hell". She had no chance of getting the business - none, nada, zero. Although she suspected the worst, she spent hours developing her proposal - unpaid consulting at it highest form. The prospect misled her (again) and she didn't know what to do.

Diagnosis: First of all, prospects don't always play it straight with salespeople. (Big surprise, right?) Basically, they'll get away with whatever they can. Who can blame them. But, prospects aren't the problem; salespeople are! First, they believe everything that the prospect tells them so when an "opportunity" presents itself, salespeople tend to think the probability of it closing is a lot higher than it really is. (Salespeople would make lousy bookies.) Second, they just don't have the guts to ask the tough questions to find out if they've got a chance to get the business. Finally, they're not sure how to broach the subject without upsetting the prospect.

Prescription: If you feel it, say it. (Gut check here.) "Mr. Prospect, I may be off base here, but I get the feeling that you've already made the decision to stay with Incumbent,

Inc. and my biggest fear is that you may need a proposal from me just because you need to have several bids, and the bottom line is I have little chance of getting your business. Is that a fair statement?"

Pay close attention to the answer, not just the words, but also the tonality and body language. Was there tacit agreement or did the prospect make a good case for your having a good chance to get the business? The prospect's job is to convince you that you <u>do</u> have a chance. If they can't convince you, you're just going to be column filler.

Now That It's Over, Can I Ask You a Question?

Problem: We blew it. The prospect said "no". We worked like crazy to put together a great presentation and our hopes for their commitment to buy were high, but it just didn't happen. The result was a no...failure, and worse, now we don't know where to go. Do we just pack it up and leave? There's got to be a better exit strategy than that.

Diagnosis: We have to look back to the qualifying steps of the call. We probably failed to accurately diagnose the prospect's pain and as a result our prescription (or proposal) was off target. But it's too late now. We need a strategy to get us back in the game. Here's an idea that works.

Prescription: After you've gotten a "no" from the prospect, try saying something like this. "Mr. Prospect, it sounds like it's over. Am I right?" Prospect acknowledges that it is. Then you say, "Well, now that it's over, can I ask you a question before I leave?" Prospect will let you do this since he has a vision of your imminent departure. You continue, "First let me apologize. I really felt like we had a good fit, but obviously I failed to completely understand what you were looking for. That's my fault." Now you conclude with, "What were you really hoping I would have brought to the table today so that you would have felt more comfortable with my proposal?"

This is where the prospect will typically bail you out and tell you what you needed to present to get the business. Once he's told you, if it's something you <u>can</u> do, you may be able to resurrect the sale by saying, "Thanks, I guess I really blew it. If I could do that, would it make any sense for us to continue talking or should we keep the file closed?" You'll be amazed at how it gets people to open up and talk, once they think it's over. It may give you that second chance you need to make the sale.

Who Pulls The Trigger?

Problem: Bob was at a meeting with the president, sales manager and the office manager of a prospective client. Prior to the meeting, Bob had figured out that the president would make the decision as long as the sales manager was positive. But, he wasn't quite sure why the office manager was at the meeting. After 30 minutes of intense discussion, the president decided that Bob's instrumentation system would greatly enhance their operation. All that needed to be resolved was the training concerns that the sales manager and office manager had expressed. Bob spent the next fifteen minutes resolving the sales manager's specific concerns. He then turned to the office manager who had not said anything throughout the entire meeting and asked, "Do you have any questions?". The office manager shyly explained that most of the questions had been answered and there were only a few minor issues. Bob enthusiastically proclaimed that the minor issues could be resolved later and sensing the opportunity to close asked, "What would you like me to do now?" The answer was, "Give us a couple of days to discuss your proposal. Call us next week."

Diagnosis: Bob assumed that the decision would be made by the president of the company and ignored the influence that the office manager could have on the decision to buy his product. The office manager, feeling ignored and uncomfortable that his concerns were not addressed, "pulled the trigger" on the sale. You can almost hear her saying to the other two after Bob left, "I don't feel good about this system. Who else is coming in?"

Prescription: You may have heard the old adage, "an involved prospect is a buying prospect." It proves to be true most of the time and it is worthwhile to ask for input from all of those involved even if you don't get much of a response. Ask each person whom you are selling at least two or three questions which require an answer and then wait for a response. It might sound like, "How do you see yourself using the (whatever)?" Or, "Bill made an excellent point earlier that I had not considered and it really helped. I sense that you may be able to help me out in the same way...", and then wait for a response. Everyone in a prospect group needs to be recognized as involved in the decision; that's why they're there. You make that happen by asking each one specific, thought provoking questions. Don't allow someone to "pull the trigger" on your sale.

Vito and Seymour*

Problem: Lisa, an account manager for a temporary staffing company, just wasn't hitting her numbers. Her industry was growing rapidly, demand for her services was clearly there, and the company was a leader in their market. She made lots of calls and, for the most part, her prospects welcomed her visits. She often brought small gifts on her visits to set herself apart from her competitors. However, the business failed to materialize. Out of frustration, Lisa sought help.

Diagnosis: Upon examination, Lisa had fallen into a pattern that eventually causes many salespeople to fail. She was not getting to the real decision maker (Vito, the Very Important Top Official). Sales 101 says that you must be in front of the decision maker.

As it turns out, Lisa had several classic problems. When she started selling in her territory, she knew the importance of being in front of Vito. But getting an appointment with Vito wasn't always so easy. Frequently, Vito asked her to see his assistant, Seymour, (aptly named since he's the data gatherer who just wants to "see more" information). Often, Seymour even said he <u>was</u> the decision maker. After this had happened a few times, Lisa saw a pattern, believed it was the norm, and decided to simply skip a step and go straight to Seymour. And since Seymour was easy to get appointments with, Lisa got more appointments. This was starting to make sense after all. Her rationale was to take the easy road. If you see enough Seymours, you'll be on the road to success. To top it off, Lisa's company, like so many others, rated her on the number of proposals she made thinking this was the key indicator of sales effectiveness. Lisa got lots of appointments, kept very busy doing proposals, but her sales didn't improve.

Prescription: Nobody said selling was easy. If it was, everyone would be successful. Seymour will only pump you for information, turn you into an "unpaid consultant", and lead you down the road to failure. Half the problems that salespeople bring to us are caused by their failure to get in front of Vito. Let Seymour help you, but you've got to sell Vito. That part is simple.

*Thanks to Tony Parinello for the Vito/Seymour concept. His book, Selling To Vito, is a good reference for anyone who sells.

Stump The Gatekeeper

Problem: Sara was becoming increasingly frustrated in her efforts to reach the decision makers when she was prospecting.   Time after time access was blocked by the gatekeepers and information gatherers.   It often seemed like there was a conspiracy to keep her from speaking to the top-level people.   She had tried various tactics, but nothing was working.   Now her sales were suffering.

Diagnosis: Gatekeepers typically feel that an important part of their job is to insulate their boss from unwanted intrusions.   Only important people are permitted to have access and salespeople are not considered important.   As for the information gatherers, they feel they've been assigned an important job.   It has two parts.   First, they need to get as much information as possible from various vendors so the company can evaluate their options.   Second, they're supposed to keep those pesky salespeople away.   These "Seemore's" feel they've been entrusted with an important job plus they want to protect their turf, so some ego is involved here as well.   But, the bottom line is that it all gets back to the negative attitude most prospects have about salespeople and that can be summed up in just a few words.   Salespeople are mainly concerned with selling something and typically bring little value to the situation.   The prospect is thinking, "Let's just get them to come in and answer our questions and then we'll decide who has the best options."

Prescription: Obviously a different approach is needed.   Here's one that works.   Ask a question they can't answer.   That's right.   Throw them a curve ball so they have to go elsewhere to get information.   For example, ask the techie a non-technical question, such as, "What type of return on investment would the company need to justify this purchase?" Or ask an administrative person a technical question like, "Can you help me understand exactly how this software will interface with your existing system?"

The questions must be real and you need to have several that the person can't answer so that he/she says, "Well, I'm not sure, Ms. ..... has that information." You could then say, "Well, without this information, I'm afraid that I can't be as responsive as I'd like to your requests. I'm concerned that I might give you information that might be inaccurate, and that would make you look bad. Does it make any sense for you to introduce me to Ms. ..... so that I can get this information first hand? Then I can be sure that I get the right information to you."

If you're having a tough time getting to the right person, try this tactic. Remember, the person asking the questions is the person who is in control.

Presenting To A Group

Problem: Darrell sold complicated software solutions to manufacturing companies. His was a complex sale in that several fact-finding meetings were typically required and the presentation often was to a group of 4-5 senior company executives. Trying to get a commitment with so many involved was difficult. He always felt like he missed presenting some important information.

Diagnosis: Selling to groups or committees is more challenging than selling to an individual. Getting a commitment when there are differing agendas, diverse personalities, and political issues involved make this type of sale very frustrating.

Prescription: Identifying the "cast of characters" early and speaking with as many of them as possible before the presentation can avoid problems. Understand who are your allies and who are possible adversaries. At the beginning of the sales presentation the introductions should be made and an agreement regarding time and meeting expectations should be set. At this point you should turn the meeting over to your principal contact to review their pain. Pay attention to the group to discern their attention level and emotional buy-in.

When the pain review has been accomplished, take back control of the meeting and validate the pain. Ask group members to elaborate as to how the pain affects their department. Demonstrate how your solutions address each pain issue and ask each person if they are 100% comfortable with your solution. Deal with exceptions before moving to the next issue. When each pain has been successfully dealt with, ask the group what the next step is.

Assuming you've done your job well, the group should close the sale themselves.

Surrogate Authority

Problem: The majority of Pamela's prospects were Fortune 1000 companies that were headquartered outside her geographic territory. Unfortunately, most of the people who had final decision-making authority on her product were at headquarters and she often had to deal with local decision influencers who could not make the final decision. She was frustrated by this situation and usually just made her presentation locally, hoping for the best. As a result, her closing rates were in the 20% range and her sales cycle was exceedingly long.

Diagnosis: Obviously, Pamela understood the importance of speaking directly to the final authority, but travel budgets and other considerations often prohibited that from happening. However, the real problem was that she lacked an effective strategy to deal with the difficulty of getting a decision from remote decision makers.

Prescription: Someone has to make a decision and the worst nightmare for a sales professional is to be denied access to the decision maker so an influencer makes your presentation for you.   Influencers typically just forward information to others with an explanation and, sometimes, a recommendation. The problem is, usually the salesperson doesn't know who is being recommended.

The solution becomes quite simple.   Promote your influencer. Yes, make your influencer the decision maker for this particular sale. Here's what to say: "I realize that the decision is made elsewhere, but here's what I'd like to do if you agree. I'd like to get from you as good an understanding of your needs as possible and then I'll offer our solution to you. When I've made the presentation, I'd like you to be able to tell me that, if the decision were yours to make, would you select my company? And by the way, I'm okay with a "no" if you think another vendor would be a better choice. Is that fair?"

This tactic is a major stroke to your prospect and requires him to get more involved in the process than he might otherwise. If he agrees to this (and he usually will), you must treat him as if he had final authority, conduct your presentation and get a "yes" or a "no" at the end. (Using a numerical scale to assess interest is an effective way to get that decision, as you know.) When the prospect sends the information to the ultimate decision maker at headquarters, it will go with his recommendation to use your product. That will improve your chances for the sale by at least 50%.

When you're confronted with an absentee decision maker, improve your chances for the sale by going the extra mile with the local contact. Make him the decision maker for a day.

.

Assign Your Prospect Some Homework

Problem: Mitch's company sold data storage solutions. A five-year veteran of selling, he called the other day for some coaching. He said that he had just completed a one-hour meeting with one of his top prospects, a large retailer who was a key prospect for his company. He explained that he had experienced difficulty getting the prospect into a discussion of pain and, when he finally did, he felt time pressure to hurry through the qualifying process. As a result, Mitch thought that he had done a poor job in the pain step. He said that this seemed typical of his meetings and that due to poor qualifying on his part, he was not closing some of the accounts that he thought he should.

Diagnosis: Unfortunately, Mitch lacked an effective way to quickly begin the pain qualification process. Without an effective tactic for getting quickly into the pain step, Mitch spent too much time building rapport and discussing inconsequential issues that only wasted both parties' time. While there were a number of tactics to find pain that Mitch had learned, none seemed to be working well for him.

Prescription: Doing the same thing and expecting different results is the definition of insanity, they say, so a new tactic was recommended. We told Mitch to add a new wrinkle to his initial meeting agreement. We suggested that he give his prospect some homework before the appointment. Mitch began saying the following to his prospects, "Mr. Prospect. In order to make our meeting as productive as possible, would you make a list of the two or three most challenging issues you are having with respect to data storage? Then we can really focus our discussion on your issues and try to develop a solution. Does that make sense?"

Interestingly enough, it did make sense to most of his prospects. When Mitch arrived at the appointment, he simply reminded the prospect about the list and asked what the issues were. From there, the pain conversation was easy to conduct. His got to the pain step quicker and was able to qualify in greater depth. He started closing more business because he understood the issues and was able to recommend better solutions.

It worked for Mitch and it will work for you. Try giving your prospect some homework before your next call.

Your Price Is <u>NOT</u> Too High

Problem: Paul, an experienced salesperson, was convinced that his company's products were overpriced. More and more he kept hearing price objections when he delivered his proposals. By his estimate at least two-thirds of his prospects complained about his prices. With this overwhelming evidence, he began to discount his prices. Although he started closing more business, his commissions weren't up significantly and his manager was becoming upset by the profitability of his accounts. He seemed to be in a devastating downward spiral. Seeking advice, most of his business associates told him to sell harder, be more convincing, and show the prospects why his products outflanked the competition. In other words, go back to the basics. But, that didn't work either.

Diagnosis: The basics were flawed. Worse than that, they weren't even valid any longer. For years we've been taught to tell our story by presenting our features, advantages and benefits. We've been taught to overcome price objections by selling value. Seemingly every sales training program out there feels there must be chapter after chapter on selling features and benefits and overcoming objections. The real reason Paul, and others, get price objections is that they continue to "pitch" their features too early (great quality, personal service, competitive prices, experienced technicians, satisfied customers, etc.). They sound like every other vendor they compete with, so the prospect perceives all vendors to be similar. Price becomes the focus.

Prescription: As they say in New York City, "Fuhget aboudit!" If you catch yourself "selling" your company early in the sales process, you're undoubtedly trying to convince your prospect that you're a qualified vendor.

Then they're qualifying you! Forget about that. It's your job to qualify them. Get good at discovering their pain, and you'll find the price objections will disappear.

The <u>Real</u> Value Of Your Features & Benefits

Problem: Qualifying is an area where salespeople often do a poor job. As a result, when the time comes for the presentation, salespeople have normally failed to discover the real issues or get any kind of serious commitment from the prospect about what will happen if he can fix the problems.

Diagnosis: Salespeople have had feature & benefit presentations drummed into their heads for years. To make matters worse, most of the training received by salespeople focuses on learning everything possible about the products and services the company offers. Sales managers are still exhorting their troops to go out and "tell our story" and "persuade them that we are the right company for them". In short, just go get the business at any cost. It shouldn't be any surprise that salespeople resort to information dumps in a desperate attempt to get a sale. Features, and their associated benefits, are meaningless to the prospect unless he has a problem that the feature addresses. If he doesn't, it's just something that can be viewed as running the price up.

Prescription: If you're absolutely compelled to talk features and benefits, try a new approach. First, take some time to really understand what problems your product or service solves and use them to begin a discussion of pain. Start thinking at the beginning of the presentation how wonderful it would be if you could tell your story about how your new ___ ___ fixes the _____ problem, about how your unique _____ helps the prospect do _____, and why your _____ was developed to overcome the _____ issue that most of your clients face. The problem is, most sales people lead with these but fail to get the prospect to acknowledge that they have the problems in the first place. It's critical to qualify properly by asking the right questions. See if they have the pains that your features address. Then set yourself up to do an effective, targeted presentation.

Here's an example. We do on-going reinforcement training because our clients tell us that they have been frustrated about spending lots of money on one or two day training events that have no lasting impact. The question to ask is, "Have you ever been concerned about spending lots of money on sending people to one or two day seminars, but seeing little or no change in their sales?" If the answer is positive, then we would probe deeper to uncover the pain associated with the issue. Having done that, in our presentation we'd discuss how our on-going reinforcement training would address their concerns about the failure of training to provide lasting results.

See how that works? Learn how to use your features and benefits to create pain.

The Incumbent Strikes Back

Problem: The deal was consummated and Troy had finally displaced his number one competitor at an important account. Having received a promise that the initial order would be sent the following week, he departed, congratulating himself on his good fortune and ability to land the tough ones. Then 3-4 days later, he received a voice mail message from his new account. From the tone of his contact's voice, he immediately knew something was wrong. Apologetically, the client told Troy that when the incumbent vendor found out that they had lost the business, they reacted with decisiveness and lowered the price significantly. The result was predictable. The initial order was cancelled and the incumbent retained the business. Having been blindsided, Troy was at a loss for what to do. His company was unwilling to match the new price and he "lost" the deal. To add insult to injury, his contact was too embarrassed to return his phone calls.

Diagnosis: Salespeople hate bad news and will go to most any length to avoid having an unpleasant discussion with a prospect. Troy was no different. His gut told him that the incumbent might react by lowering their price, but he didn't want to face that possibility and didn't know how to deal with it anyway.

Prescription: You've got to deal with landmines early in the process. Certainly the potential for the incumbent to cut price or make some other compelling concession to keep the business always exists. The successful salesperson needs a tactic to deal with this eventuality. Risky though it sounds, Troy should have met the threat head on before he left the meeting with his "new client". He might have said, "I'm kind of curious. What do you think your present supplier will do when they find out you've decided to give us your business?" Often the prospect will respond by saying that they might, indeed, lower their price in order to keep the business. At that point the only response the salesperson should make is to say, "Assuming they do lower their price, what will you do?" Had Troy brought up the subject himself he would have been in control of the situation instead of being in a reactive mode.

When the issue is raised, the prospect will respond in only one of two ways. If they were making the change because of sincere dissatisfaction with the incumbent, they typically will decline to accept concessions. Once having told the salesperson that, the likelihood of it happening is remote. However, if they say that they may have to pay attention to concessions, the sale was never made in the first place. That being so, the salesperson is still there and can continue the sales process.

The sale is not made until the money is in your bank account, so keep your eyes open for things that can go wrong, especially the obvious ones.

Leave Your Agenda
At The Office

Problem: Alligator Software had just introduced a major revision to their software but, in spite of tremendous initial enthusiasm, sales fell far short of expectations and management started to receive complaints about the conduct of their overzealous salespeople.

Diagnosis: Alligator was proud of their newest revisions, so much so that management was convinced that they were finally in a position to overtake their primary competitor who owned 60% of the market. A national sales meeting was held and the entire forty person sales team converged on San Diego for a quick one and a half day meeting to introduce the "new product". After the proud techies got their chance to demo the software, the marketing department spent a half-day helping the salespeople understand all the features and benefits and how the new product would help their prospects reach new levels of efficiency.

Finally, management got their chance and did they ever turn on the motivation! With extraordinary zeal they introduced the new compensation plan for sales and it was generous, to say the least. They left the salespeople with this message: "The market is ready for this product. It's new and innovative and everybody needs it. We've invested megabucks in development and need to recoup our investment. So get out there and move it. Don't take no for an answer. You can make it happen!"

So the highly motivated sales force departed, full of high expectations and renewed enthusiasm, but with the wrong agenda.

How easily we forget! It's not about you. It's about your prospect. Alligator's sales force descended on their unwary prospects like a bunch of wild animals intent on the kill. Their attitude was...forget about what the prospect needs, we've got to sell this stuff, now. Consultative selling went by the wayside and the vultures showed up. And, nobody bought.

Prescription: Simple. Shut up and listen. People aren't buying because you've got a quota or because your management said to go out and move the product. Here's what Ray Smith, the former Chairman and CEO of Bell Atlantic has to say about salespeople:

"The great sales professional helps you eliminate issues that are not a problem, and then focus you in on the really critical dimensions of the situation. At the right moment, the good ones ask the right questions. You don't want someone peddling a solution that comes with an agenda, which many do."

Alligator's sales force came with an agenda – move the product. That was their focus on every call. They cared little about the prospect's issues and asked few questions. They were clearly under pressure and it showed. Their prospects felt like they were being pressured to buy a used car or a time share and they didn't buy. People buy for their reasons, not yours, so stop selling and start listening.

It's "Never" Price

Problem: One of the most common objections salespeople get is about price: "That's a bit more than we were thinking about paying." "Your prices are kind of high." "That just doesn't fit our budget" are typical comments. Salespeople tend to be very aggressive in their attempts to overcome price objections and begin dropping their price to get the sale. And, more often than not, once the price issue has been "resolved", another objection comes to the surface. Sometimes it seems to be a never-ending circle of objections from the prospect.

Diagnosis: Prospects may use the price objection as an excuse not to buy when, in fact, the real reason is different. Think about it. You've probably said on more than one occasion, "That's more than I wanted to spend", when what you really meant was it doesn't have the functionality you were looking for or the style just wasn't right. Or because you had no real conviction that solution will work and even under the best circumstances you probably wouldn't buy it. Sometimes price objections are real and sometimes they're smokescreens. Your job is to figure it out correctly.

Prescription: The first thing you must do when you hear a price objection is to make sure that it's the real issue. You want to isolate it so that you don't have to deal with any other issues later on. So, ask the prospect this question: "I don't know why this is, but typically when we hear the price is too high, it's something else in the proposal that someone didn't like and not necessarily the price. Is that the case here?"

Now the prospect has two alternatives: they can tell you what the real objection is or they can say that everything else is fine and it really is just about price. If it's something other than price, you must deal with that. If it really is price, you should find out how far apart you are and determine whether or not you want to be responsive. Assuming you have some flexibility, ask them what would happen if you were able to reach agreement on price. If their answer is anything other than "we'll have a deal", you need to do more qualifying or consider walking.

Isolating the objection is very important so you can deal with the real issue(s). Secondarily, when the prospect declines the opportunity to be critical of other issues in the proposal, they usually start to tell you what they liked and why. When that happens, they're starting to sell themselves and that helps you diffuse the price issue.

Let The Prospect Eliminate His Own Objections

Problem: Kelly's company had developed a training program for their customers (and prospects) that was designed to position them as a leader in their industry, enable their customers to use their technology more effectively and reduce emergency calls to the tech support department. Kelly was having difficulty determining why one of his largest customers was not moving forward on enrolling his people in this important training program sponsored by his company. Granted, the training was not free, but at $995 per person it had the potential to save his client many thousands of dollars per year. He had already determined that the customer was concerned about the high number of incidents of faulty applications that the training program was developed to address, so there was significant pain. Basically, this seemed to be a "no brainer". But, Kelly just couldn't figure out why he couldn't get the deal closed and it was clear that, unless he was able to get to the root of the problem, the idea would die a slow death.

Diagnosis: Often prospects don't know the specific reasons why they don't want to move forward. They know they're uncomfortable with something, but they just can't seem to put their finger on it. So they stall, saying things like "We just haven't had time to make the decision yet" or "How about calling me back in a few days". We've all been there and, as we know, time kills deals so we need to find a way to get the objection(s) to the surface so we can deal with them.

Prescription: Put yourself in the prospect's shoes. Try to come up with two or three of the objections that you think he is having. In Kelly's case, the assumption was two things: the prospect didn't have the conviction that the training would solve the problem or the money was just not available to train the people. So, Kelly said the following, "Fred, obviously you're having some difficulty moving forward with the training program. I'm guessing it has to be because you're either not convinced the training will be effective or that the budget just isn't available for you to move forward. Which one is it?

By raising the objections himself, Kelly has put the prospect in a position where he must deal with them. He either has to agree that they are issues, or eliminate them himself. If the objections are valid, they can discuss them and move forward. Give the prospect some "objection" options, and let him eliminate them so you can keep the sales process moving forward.

Getting Objections?
Try A Role Reversal

Problem: Objections are probably the most misunderstood area of selling and typically salespeople are not very good at dealing with them.

Diagnosis: Experience tells us that objections are really not "buying signals" like the sales gurus of old have told us. In fact, objections could be deal breakers if we don't handle them properly so most salespeople would rather not deal with them at all. Traditional methods of handling objections (memorizing ten ways to defeat the price objection, etc.) are not real world solutions for most salespeople. They can't remember most of them under pressure anyway, so avoidance becomes the strategy.

Prescription: If you keep doing things the way you've always done them, you'll get the same results. In Common Sense Selling we want the salesperson to introduce the objections. It's the prospect's job to resolve them. If this sounds like we've got it backwards well, in a sense we do. In the real world, if you've got a ticking time bomb on the table, it's better to disarm it before it blows up.

Here's an example. Let's assume you know your prospect has had a problem with your company in the past. You're very concerned that this bad experience will be brought up by the prospect and used as a reason not to use you again. Typically, the salesperson would prefer to "let sleeping dogs lie" and avoid discussing it. However, the potential still clearly exists for the prospect to raise the issue later and use it as a bargaining tool. ("Yes, but we've had a problem with you guys in the past and you'll have to significantly lower your prices before we would even consider....".) Sound familiar?

A more effective way to deal with this issue is to bring the problem up early by saying, "I'm told you had a bad experience with our company a couple of years ago. My biggest concern is that it's still an issue for you. Do we need to spend a few minutes discussing it before we ...?" If the prospect says it still is an issue, your response would be, "If it's still an issue, I'm curious as to why you'd even want to meet with me. Can you help me with that?" Let's face it, there's got to be some pain involved because most prospects have better things to do with their time than to have you come in for a tongue lashing.

If it's no longer an issue, you'll be told that. Now you can focus on the prospect's pain and not be worried about past problems. Either way, we take control of the situation and deal with it.

What stalls or objections do you get on a regular basis? Can you use this tactic to deal with them more effectively?

.

You Don't Need To Respond To Statements

Problem: You spent the better part of a day putting together a proposal and preparing for a big presentation. You're ready for your scheduled meeting and finally get your chance. Everything goes great and you are at that point waiting for the buyer to say, "Yes". The prospect warmly smiles and says, "That was one of the best presentations that I have had. Your product really solves our problem nicely..." You want to relax but anticipate one last objection. The prospect continues with the warm smile and states, "But your prices are more than we had anticipated spending." You are ready and say "I really want to get your business so I will take off 10% if we can complete it today." "Thanks, I appreciate that", your prospect responds as he signs the PO.

Diagnosis: Prospects are taught to manipulate salespeople. Was the prospect's statement about your pricing intended to manipulate you into reducing your price or was it just an innocent comment? Based on how this sales call ended we can only speculate.

It is astounding how often a salesperson will automatically assume that statements are objections. You don't have to answer statements! One of the basic tactics taught in just about every negotiating seminar is "the flinch". For example: seller states the price, buyer reacts physically with a shrug or grimace and makes a statement ("Wow, that's kind of high.") It works like magic on salespeople.

If you want to see how easy it is to manipulate a salesperson, go to any car dealership, get a price on a car and state "Wow, that's high!" Assuming you stare and say nothing after that initial statement, 90% of salespeople will either start to redo the numbers or defend his price.

Prescription: When a prospect makes a statement that sounds like an objection, simply ask, "Which means...?", and then wait silently and look puzzled. Don't cave in and don't get defensive. Let the prospect make the next move. It might surprise you. If you want to know why a statement was made, you have to ask the prospect a question. Don't assume.

The Price Trap

Problem: One of the most frequent complaints we hear from business owners, sales managers and salespeople alike is the following: "Price is the primary focus of the sale these days -- all of our prospects want the lowest price." It starts out innocently enough. Buyers lead with questions and comments like these: "How much is it? Can you give me a quote?" As the sales discussion proceeds it gets more intense: "That seems like a lot." or "Why is it so expensive?" or "I saw it for less." Salespeople often respond by cutting price thus giving away margins and commissions.

Diagnosis: People who sell hear about price so often that they expect the conversation to dwell on price and they tend to overreact to price concerns. Sixty-eight percent of salespeople from a wide range of industries thought that price was the main concern of the customer based on a recent survey conducted by The Sales Board. In contrast, when customers were asked what was most important to them in a purchase their response was much different. The majority of people were more concerned with quality, service and relationship than price.

Prescription: To get out of the price trap, you have to stop focusing on it. The only time price is the main issue is when there are no other factors that are important which is rarely (maybe never) the case. The next step is to differentiate yourself and your product so that the prospect does not focus on price. That means not giving feature and benefit presentations -- which cause you to look like every other salesperson.

Instead, change your approach in a couple of ways to focus on the prospect and her challenges and not on your product.

First, suggest to your prospect that it's important to establish an environment where you can explore the details about the prospect's situation. Mention to the prospect that your "biggest concern" is that her focus will be on price and that addressing the real issues (pain) will take a back seat to price. By addressing the price issue early on, she will tell you where price fits into the decision-making criteria. Experience shows that it will become secondary if you are successful in refocusing the discussion to the prospect's pain. Next, lead an interactive discussion to understand the emotional reasons behind the prospect's situation and uncover the pains that need to be addressed. By doing this you and the prospect will mutually discover if there is value in your product and remove the emphasis on price.

Straight Talk From The Authors

Selling is a serious business, yet most salespeople treat it as if it was a temporary career stopover. The wonderful thing about selling is that it offers unlimited income to those who are really good, a real opportunity to help people, solve problems, and a sense of independence that is lacking in many other pursuits. If you possess exceptional selling skills, you have all the job security in the world.

We strongly encourage you to take your profession seriously. To be the best, enroll yourself in a training program that teaches the skills you'll need to succeed in the kind of selling that you do. Books are fine, audio tapes are okay too, and so are the one-day motivational programs that are available from the celebrity trainers. But they alone won't take you to the head of the class. Enroll yourself in a training program that offers reinforcement and coaching. Do something every week to increase your knowledge of selling so that you can stay current with the latest strategies and tactics. This will enable you to stay at the top of your game (profession). CPA's and physicians are required to take continuing education courses to maintain their licenses; selling should be no different.

If you're interested in finding someone in your local area who offers this type of on-going reinforcement training, we would be pleased to suggest a qualified trainer close to you.

About the Authors

Jim Dunn and John Schumann are the principals of SalesCoach, LLC. Both have extensive experience selling, managing sales forces and training salespeople. Their approach to the sales process is a combination of the best practices in selling today.

Products Available from SalesCoach

Computer Based Training Programs

Why Salespeople Struggle (Self-Inflicted Problems and Common Sense Solutions) $49.95

Learn how and why buyers seem to control the sales process (and your success); how to avoid "unpaid consulting"; learn a new selling system based on common sense that really works.

Proactive Cold Calling Strategies $49.95

Discover what's wrong with the way 90% of salespeople (even experienced ones) make cold calls; learn a new introductory pain probe that will make you sound totally different from all the other salespeople who are competing for your prospect's time; practice making cold calls using our exclusive cold calling simulator.

Damage Control (Dealing With Stalls, Objections & Roadblocks) $49.95

Find out why the traditional methods of handling stalls and objections don't work; learn a set of innovative tactics to deal with the 12 most common stalls and objections that salespeople hear; practice your new tactics in our exclusive sales simulator.

Becoming A World Class Qualifier $49.95

The best qualifiers are the most effective closers. Designed for the complex sale, this program will teach you how to ask the right questions to determine your prospect's real buying motivation, budgets and decision process. You'll be able to practice these new skills using our exclusive sales simulator.

Audiotapes and CD's

Quick Lessons & Role Plays $39.95

Over one hour of fast-paced advice and role plays on topics like qualifying, cold calling, handling stalls and objections, setting meeting agreements, asking for referrals, and much more. This audio CD takes learning from the theoretical to the practical. There's nothing like it on the market today.

Order Today!

Call (800) 235-2816

Ask for the SalesCoach Order Desk.